Influencer Relations

Insights on Analyst Value

Duncan Chapple & Sven Litke

Second edition

FOLRSE
PRESS

Second edition, 2018

ISBN 978-0-906378-08-3
This collection © Kea Company 2018.

Published by Folrose Press.

Printed in the United Kingdom by Lightning Source.

Table of Contents

Introduction

Bob Sakakeeny

Gartner, Colony, McGovern, Anderson, Johnson, Willmott, Matlack, Norman. When I started working with analyst firms over 35 years ago, they were small enough that you often dealt with the founder and other principals. They were not only heads of research but also the firms' primary sales people.

Analyst Relations was mostly distributed across the company and seldom done by a dedicated staff. Legacy systems were massive iron ovens, innovation was done on "mini" computers, and the emerging disruptive technology was called a PC (P for professional, not personal). My first sale included a 60 MB disk drive with a 15 MB removable drive, which had to be moved with a forklift and cost over $10,000.

It is almost trite to say that things have changed for both the analyst firms and the vendors. As I've moved back and forth from being an analyst's client to being an analyst, I've been able to see the good, the bad and the ugly of both sides.

Whether sizing current or potential markets, assessing disruptive technologies and services, helping a client prepare for critical presentations, or focused primary and secondary market research, or doing competitive analysis, vendors and analysts need to partner with each other for each to succeed. Like it or not, analysts do influence what and how users buy what vendors offer. For every $100 spent by users, analysts have influenced $15-$25 of that spending.

The same technology that analysts opine about has also changed the way analysts and their clients interact. But, technology has also moved us from having a dearth of information to a surfeit of information. As the kids say, TMI! As the old fart says, can't separate the wheat from the chaff. Analysts can be effective in reducing the noise and helping to focus on what is important.

The beauty of this book is that while helping the reader understand how to work with analysts, it also is critical to understanding why you must work with analysts. Duncan and Sven are expert practitioners and know what it takes to do AR for all types and sizes of companies.

They are also expert trainers and teachers, who can share their knowledge and expertise in a variety of ways. They have made their knowledge very accessible in this book, so you can consume it in one sitting or in bite-sized bits. Whatever your style, read the book and use it to map out your company's AR strategy – which includes making sure the "suits and the skirts" understand why AR is at least as important as IR and PR.

Robert "Bob" Sakakeeny is a Partner at Kea Company. He has 35 years experience in the high technology industry spanning senior roles in analyst firms and high technology providers. As a research director in what is now Gartner, he created and grew a new service which covered network devices, network operating systems and networking protocols. In addition to several years building analyst relations at Hewlett Packard, he managed competitive intelligence and business strategy at CA Technologies, EMC, and Wang Laboratories.

Preface

Duncan Chapple

One of the biggest changes Sven Litke and I have seen since we joined the information, communications and technology (ICT) industry in the 1990s has been the growing influence of industry analysts. Firms like Gartner and Ovum, where we used to work, and other third-party advisors influence a large minority of technology buying, and a majority of the largest ICT purchases by enterprises.

Our book aims to take a new approach to analysts and how the providers of ICT solutions can benefit from their insight and influence. There are some excellent books on analyst relations which have been warmly received. Our colleague Efrem Mallach's invaluable landmark book, Win them Over: a guide to consultant and analyst relations, is now in its third edition. Ralf Leinemann and I co-authored a companion volume aimed at managers familiar with media relations, Industry Analyst Relations: An Extension to Public Relations, which has been one of the top-selling AR books on Amazon for several years. In addition to Ralf's German-language book on AR, co-authored with members of the Deutscher Analyst Relations Arbeitskreis, volumes by Louis Columbus, Geoff Roach, Lisa Perry and Richard Stiennon have made notable contributions. Unlike those volumes, this is not an introduction to AR: this is a book for practitioners, focussed on emergent challenges like the rise of freemium analyst firms, the broadening value proposition of analysts and the appearance of automated research driven by user reviews.

Also unlike other books, this volume is structured in five chapters corresponding to our IDEAL framework for analyst relations: Every part of an analyst/consultant relations program fits one of the five IDEAL categories:

1. **Identify refers to identifying your analyst/consultant relations targets, both in terms of the relevance of individual analysts and the value they have for your clients. As a category of activity, it also includes planning the program: identifying what needs to be done.**
2. **Drive refers to putting measurable programs in place that will drive operational excellence.**
3. **Execute is carrying out the program activities, engaging with analysts and consultants.**
4. **Align means aligning what you do with corporate messages and strategies.**
5. **Leverage is taking advantage of analyst/consultant relations to bring value to your company, leveraging your relationships for strategic benefit. That makes your program a strategic adjunct to business development. That is your goal.**

Finally, this book differs in that is is in every way a collective effort. Although Sven and I have written much of the book, a team of people has contributed to the ideas in it. Several sections have author's bylines. Countless others have contributed to our ideas. We want to especially thank Andrew Reed, Annelieke Nagel, Anthony Kennada, Bram Weerts, Christopher Manfredi, Derk Erbé, Donna Stein, Efrem Mallach, Emily Almond,

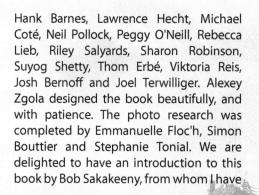

Hank Barnes, Lawrence Hecht, Michael Coté, Neil Pollock, Peggy O'Neill, Rebecca Lieb, Riley Salyards, Sharon Robinson, Suyog Shetty, Thom Erbé, Viktoria Reis, Josh Bernoff and Joel Terwilliger. Alexey Zgola designed the book beautifully, and with patience. The photo research was completed by Emmanuelle Floc'h, Simon Bouttier and Stephanie Tonial. We are delighted to have an introduction to this book by Bob Sakakeeny, from whom I have learned so much both as a client and now as one of our partners in Kea Company. There are too many others to mention: in particular we celebrate our clients, who have challenged us to develop our Analyst Value Survey and use it as the lighthouse to guide our work, and the participants in our annual forum at King's College London where so many of the ideas in this book have been developed and tested.

Since working as an analyst and consultant at Ovum, Europe's largest analyst firm, Duncan Chapple has been the preeminent researcher worldwide into analyst value and analyst relations effectiveness. He held senior analyst relations roles at what are now Ketchum, Deloitte, Speed Communications and Octopus Group. He founded Lighthouse Analyst Relations, which joined Kea Company in 2013.

Identify

Which analysts matter

Which influencers are most relevant?

One of the more common inquiries that Kea Company handles is "How can I know which analysts are most relevant? Should I focus on traditional influencers or put some effort toward these new style influencers?"

With many more players on the influencer landscape it is hard for vendors and analyst relations (AR) teams to determine who to focus on when it comes to planning and resource allocation.

A technique that very few vendors and AR teams use is asking customers and prospects about where they turn for advice about IT strategy and hardware/software/services purchasing decisions. Why do so few use this technique? First, this technique is rarely used because it is not top of mind with most AR professionals. Second and most important, this is a non-trivial exercise that requires political capital, best practices, labor, and potentially budget.

Whenever a Kea Company strategist suggests that AR should ask customers and prospects about their sources of advice we typically see the proverbial light bulb go on over the AR manager's head. This light bulb burns bright for a few seconds and then flickers finally going dark as the AR manager focuses on the work required. While on the surface asking customers might seem like too much work, we think that AR needs to seriously consider adding this technique to its portfolio.

The business value of asking customers is very high including:

▸ **Selling effectiveness:** Knowing who prospects turn to for advice can help sales professionals be better prepared to deal with that influence

▸ **Planning:** Knowing who customers actually turn to for advice can reprioritize – sometimes radically – which analysts and other influencers AR should consider most relevant and most important

▸ Enhancing executive sponsorship: The insights from customers and prospects can help executives and other stakeholders understand the impact of analysts on sales and lead to active sponsorship instead of passive support

There are four basic ways AR can ask customers about their sources of information and advice:

1. **AR itself does a survey of the company's customers and (potentially) prospects** DIY
2. **AR hires a third-party firm to conduct the survey of the company's customers and (potentially) prospects** 3rd pty
3. **Participate in a third-party multi-vendor survey of buyers**
4. **AR teams requests that their sales colleagues ask customers and pass that information to AR** Sales

Each of these approaches has pluses and minuses that will make them more or less attractive depending on the situation. Kea Company can advise clients on this technique, provide sample surveys, train sales reps how to ask customers about influencers and such.

Kea Company Advice:

▸ The AR strategic and tactical plan should have an initiative for asking customers about their sources of information and advice

▸ Surveys should look at both information and advice separately and within the context of the entire sales cycle

▸ Working with sales representatives to gain customer intelligence should be done within the framework of an AR-Sales Partnership program

Bottom Line: Gaining intelligence from customers about their sources of information and advice is a great addition to AR planning and execution. While this technique does require some effort and expense, the information and insights are extremely valuable.

Frustrated Customers Produce Opportunities for Upstart Analyst Firms

"Everything that has been disseminated for free this past year has been excellent. Gartner and Forrester material is either dated, too high level, not believable, or tailored to small companies only."

This comment to the Analyst Value Survey from a senior manager in one of the world's biggest enterprises really struck the same note as many other users of analyst services. While some analyst firms are seen as hard to work with or increasingly rigid, for example Gartner with workgroup pricing and limiting the ability of clients' colleagues to listen in on calls, some other firms are seen as being easier partners to work, having more actionable insight, or compelling (dare we even say entertaining) content.

Many users are reporting much higher satisfaction with firms that are seen as being more interactive, community-oriented and engaging. Alsbridge, HfS and ISG are mentioned. Indeed, it's fair to say that in this year's survey we see real enthusiasm from both suppliers and enterprises that there are now really promising complementary providers.

We're also starting to see the impact of free research. Many respondents are in firms that have limited their number of employees able to access the major analyst houses, producing the intriguing scenario that free research might be used more widely in some organisations that the analyst firms it subscribes to. It's now possible to be expert user of analysts, and to know the analysts and their firms well, but not actually have a subscription. Generally, of course, that's not the case: Most respondents are Gartner subscribers. However, their monopoly on a premium customer experience might be slipping.

That shift towards plurality is especially driven by the development of cloud solutions and outsourcing services across the entire IT and telecoms world. Services analysts and sourcing advisors seem to have a finger in every pie. As one respondent explained, "the challenge that both the analysts and the advisory firms have is the broad rapidly changing technology in the marketplace. The decision they have to make is to limit their focus or grow their practice in order to cover all of these areas." That seems to be pushing people to refine their investment in analyst firms in two ways: either to identify individual analysts rather than firms to have strategic relationships with; or to find one firm that can cover all their needs.

Of course the more extensive coverage of the market by Gartner, Forrester and IDC is not their only advantage. Gartner, for example, has three sales people for every analyst: a ratio that other analyst firms would be well advised to follow. A wide range of coverage areas isn't always better for every client, especially if you have a question that three of four analysts have different parts of the answer to, leaving you to make sense of them.

Gartner's leadership in market share will be hard to erode while it continues not only to have sales leadership but also deliver better value for money than other large analyst firms. It is also mistaken to think that the other analyst firms that are performing well in the Analyst Value Survey are all getting the same things right.

Second tier risers
Source: Analyst Value Survey, 2016

Blue Hill Research
PA Consulting
Enderle
G2 Crowd
Diginomica
InfoTrends
LNS
Technology Evaluation Centers
VDC Research
VentureBeat
Wikibon

A great illustration of that is the chart above, which shows the firms we're most likely to add into the survey next year (we're too polite to talk about the ones they will replace, especially since many of those are respected national leaders with little regional or global traction). While we aim to include in the survey every firm with more than a dozen full-time analysts, we see that there are some smaller firms that have a notable level of market impact. TechMarketView is a great example of that, and we're also seeing firms with more innovative business models, like BI Intelligence, and with niche leadership, like insurance analysts Novarica.

Who Are They?
Identifying
the Influencers
of Today and Tomorrow

*M*ost people trying to reach a decision for a vendor, a product or a service will try to get at least a couple of third party opinions on the downsides or benefits of any particular choice. In addition to recommendations from friends and business partners the world's influencers are often key-components in this process.

So far so good, but when you are planning to engage with these influencers the first step is to identify them. For any given topic there usually is a vast pool of relevant people to take into account. This not only includes the top journalists and tier 1 industry analysts but also various other potential influencers in the market. Among the obvious candidates are consultants, associations and bloggers but it might also be worth to think about the account managers and client relation people supporting your potential customers in their interactions with the analyst firms.

A good way to get started is to review what is being said about your market niche in the various social media groups, blogs, Tweets and magazines. By checking the number of replies, comments and page views you will get a good first impression of the market reach and interest the topic has. Also it is well worth checking the published research by the leading analyst companies to see what trends are shaping the market and who is covering these topics. In addition you can use the search engines to check the key sources in the web and their relevance in the eyes of the search engines. Also don't forget to talk to your customers and prospects to get some feedback on how they have come across your company and products and what information sources they use to reach a buying decision. The combination of these efforts will probably yield a long list of people who have something to say about your area of interest.

To narrow down the list of influencers to target you will first have to decide what you want to achieve with your influencer marketing activities. For this purpose it makes sense to create "influencer rating cards" to rank the influencer depending on various criteria. The choice and importance of these criteria obviously depends on the goals you have set for your influencer marketing activities. Examples for potential criteria are market reach, thought leadership, geographical coverage, page views, number of followers etc. Gathering this information will take up some time but it pays to get it right to make sure you spend your (limited) time on the right audience. To speed up the identification and ranking process it might make sense for you to involve an influencer marketing agency who already has some background information or an influencer database with the relevant metrics. At the end of this process you should end up with a list of 5-15 key influencers relevant for your market with whom you can start your influencer marketing activities. But keep in mind – things will change over time with influencers changing their focus, losing audience and new influencers appearing in the market. This means you will have to continuously review and update your list.

Did Apple and IBM Know Which Analysts Could Trash Share Prices? Do You?

*Y*ou probably don't know all the investor-savvy analysts pushing down tech share prices. Apple's shocking $40bn share price fall in through September and mid-October 2015 wasn't simply about actors' privacy. And the $20bn wiped off IBM's share price on October 18 wasn't just about sluggish sales.

These were some of a number of tech firms that suffered major financial blows in just six months, including most of 2012's major IPOs. The impact can be lasting: IBM's value fell 10 percent, while both the market as a whole, reflected by the Dow and S&P 500, and competitors like Microsoft, HP and Cisco was up by more than 7 percent.

We think most other AR teams are flying blind. Sadly CFO's don't have industry analysts on their radar. Expect more crashes.

In a nutshell

Most investor relations programs target sell-side equity analysts, often more than investors themselves, and rarely reach out to industry analysts. That means that industry analysts offer a valuable second opinion, free from financial spin, and are increasing used by finance professionals. It also means that financial analysts are under-informed about private firms' business models, and industry analysts are often called in to advise funds and VCs on start-ups

Sadly, few influencer relations professionals know which analysts influence analysts, or how spokespeople can speak finance – rather than features – to them.

As a result, the current slide in stock prices is exposing most exchange-listed tech and telecoms firms to a substantial repetitional danger with an associated financial risk that's widely overlooked. Private firms are also missing out on the opportunity to influence analysts who are

more on industry analysts than banks do. Because start ups have useless multiples, investors are increasingly worried that their funds have nowhere to go if the market tumbles.

Analysts are central to that. While investment banks have always used analysts, and many analyst firms are rooted in supplying insight to investors, our Analyst Value Survey shows a remarkable shift. The freemium and vendor-sponsored model couples with analysts' growing media profile (both social and earned) to multiply analysts' impact on investors. Central to Apple's fall was Gartner's statement downplaying the market for tablets just as the new iPads were launched.

speaking to their potential investors, or the firms that represent them.

Context

Investors are moving from cautious to nervous. First funding rounds are increasingly hard for tech firms. There is more late round funding because IPOs are getting rarer. Box and other bellwethers are coming under increasing scrutiny. Friendly bankers are running to get to out, and offload to pension funds. In term that means there are more private buyers, buyers who use their own stock and rely

The most dangerous months have also been remarkable for a series of analyst reports talking down IBM's chances in several market sectors, including CMS, Cloud, databases, and integration.

This shows a new context: AR is increasingly for sales of distressed companies rather than of solutions. Analysts are now also being asked: who could investors sell their holdings in tech firms to, or who can they buy?

"Deal-Maker or Breaker" is over & Other Harsh AR Truths

Breakout year was 2014 for freemium analyst firms. It's fundamentally ended the fantasy that only Gartner and Forrester were "deal-maker or breaker" firms. An excellent illustration of that is the data from the Analyst Value Survey. The chart below shows the firms where the demand-side and supply-side respondents gave the most different answers to the question: which firms most influence buyers?

Here's how to understand the chart, first in terms of meaning, and second in term of method:

▶ **Meaning**. In the opinion of people on the demand-side, firms like Aberdeen and DCG have substantially more influence on buyers than the supply-side admits, and Gartner and IDC have substantially less influence on buyers than the supply-side thinks.

▶ **Method**. Firms that are higher up were more often said to be more

Under- and over-estimation of analyst firms by vendors
Source: InfluencerRelations.com/3524

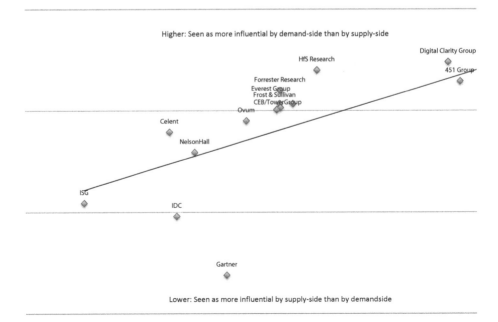

influential on buyers by people on the demand-side than buy people on the supply side (it's the absolute gap between the scores given by those two groups, not the absolute scores). The horizontal axis shows the ratio between those numbers, and you can ignore that for now. If you want the run the numbers yourself, you can buy the AVS here.

Gartner and Forrester are, as always, the firms that are said to be most influential. But there's a difference between the demand- and supply-side in how strongly they see that leadership. Some firms are substantially under-estimated by the supply-side: Aberdeen, DCG, HfS, 451, Datamonitor and Forrester. Suppliers are not putting enough effort into those overlooked firms.

One example: 30% of supply-side people say IDC influences buyers, but only 20% on the demand-side. Over 21% of people on the demand-side say HfS Research influence buyers, but only 17% on the supply side. So, if most firms put twice as much AR effort into IDC than into HfS, but HfS is actually more influential then that is lost opportunity.

As Tolstoy might have said, all overlooked analyst firms are different: Aberdeen is not an analyst in our opinion, but a research firm delivering content services. DCG and HfS are freemium firms. 451 and Datamonitor have weak business development aimed at vendors (and vendors can't address themselves to Datamonitor's tech-agnostic expertise in energy, healthcare, finance and consumer goods).

These lost opportunities are not occurring for simple reasons. Nor are they easy to turn around: Aberdeen, for example, is hardly open to non-client influence. But they reflect a real perception gap, and some wasted effort that needs to be shifted.

Of course this picture will be different for each industry: services is the major part of the industry now, but services analyst firms might not be influential in an equipment segmen.

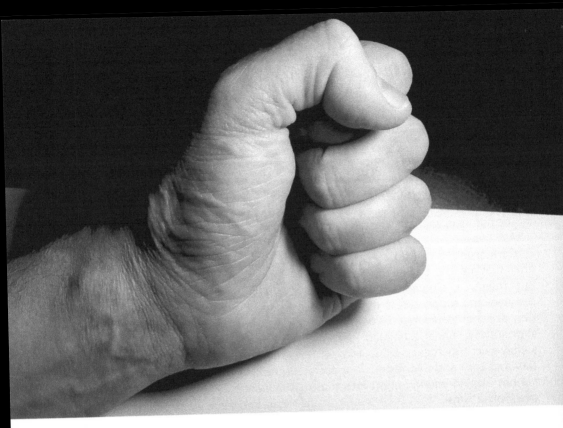

The New Industry Analysts, Again

Michael Coté

NEVER MIND JOURNALISM, IT'S INDUSTRY ANALYSTS WHO ARE BEING DISRUPTED

I keep coming across a new crop of IT industry analysts who end up getting compared incorrectly to journalists. It's little wonder as most people have little idea what an industry analyst does; it's not like analysts, hidden behind their austere paywalls, help much there.

People like Horace Dediu, Ben Thompson, and others are experimenting with ways to disrupt industry analysts. They're using new business models and tools that often seem bonkers to the more traditional analysts wrapped up all warm and tight in their blue blazers.

Their models focus on narrow topics with broad appeal (Apple, vendor sports among high profile tech companies [you can call this "strategy"], and "social") and they tend to make much, if not all, of their content free. What they lack is the breadth of the overall industry analyst world (they have no opinion on what type of identity and access management or CRM system you might want to use), but that can could be fixed as more "independent" analysts like themselves pop up. There's also not a lot of "short-listing" (ranking of vendors and products intended to be used by IT decision makers and buyers) that these folks do; this an area where incumbents can easily defend themselves.

One way of looking at it is the "consumerization of industry analysis:" focusing on selling and serving individuals rather than enterprises. Indeed, current industry analyst shops sell mostly to companies and are near impossible for individuals to work with.

IMAGINE BEN THOMPSON TIMES 50

While Horace is patient zero here, the best example of this trend in action is Ben Thompson, or "stratechery." For whatever reason – and his self-proclaimed Midwestern modestly would make him blush at this notion – he talks about his business more and, thus, provides a better view into the business side of this trend.

In the first episode of his podcast, Ben lays out the model he's trying to execute (and how, you know, the Internet and blogging makes all this possible); he later elaborated on it with his rain forest layer cake metaphor; and in an even more recent episode goes over how his business has evolved.

How well do these models work? Well, we have some data points from Ben since he's discussed his momentum by subscriber numbers a few times. Let's compare it to what I've made as analyst over the years to get a sense of what's "normal":

This excludes a lot of thing: health insurance is the biggest and other non-cash compensation.

The point is to show that at the individual level, Ben is doing well. His business is performing well compared to what's "normal" for analysts. The recent growth rate looks even more promising. I actually ended up at the high end of the analyst wage chart (I think). The average is a lot closer to $100,000 the more junior you get.

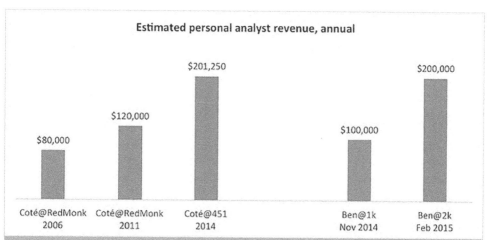

Estimated personal analyst revenue, annual

Sources: my often shoddy memory [adding up salary and bonus approximations], and Ben Thompson talking about reaching 1,000 subscribers on November 13th, 2014, and then 2,000 on February 2nd, 2015

If this model can be replicated by other individuals, we'll see the biggest disruption to the industry analyst business since the Web. What the established firms have is marketing reach, brand awareness, and lots of money and time. The first two are hard for individuals to achieve, but not impossible. The last two are harder.

I think there's a lot of room for Gartner (the mega firm) and the RedMonks (boutique firms) of the world, but in the middle things will get harder. Forrester is always rearing to be a #2, but revenue-wise, they have a long way to go; IDC will probably keep winching the cost-cranks and double down on being Master of the PivotTable. My former friends at 451 Research have a lot of potential, but like all the other folks in the middle, they need to keep honing their strategies and go-to-market. I keep hearing that HfS is awesome, which could provide an interesting case.

With that bucket of points made for the tl;dr crowd, the rest is an extended treatment.

THE ENTERPRISE GRUBER

I ran into Nick Muldoon a few years ago at a DevOpsDays (in 2012, right in the middle of my time at Dell) and he paid me a high compliment, loosely quoted from memory: "I always thought you could be the Gruber of enterprise IT." Indeed, that's what all my type dream about when we drive past those lottery billboards on the way to the airport at 4:30am: sitting at home, reading news, blogging, and being so awesome that it pays well.

To some extent, I did that at RedMonk; not at Dell, for sure: there's no talking in public, really, when you work on strategy and M&A. And I did that on the pay side of the paywall at 451 Research. I loved it: writing up what I think about the IT industry targeted at helping my "audience" (we called them "clients") make better decisions about IT, be it product management,

competing, investing, or using IT. (There's a minority that look towards analysts for entertainment, which is valid, but likely pays poorly.)

In part, that's what I've been asked to do in my new job at Pivotal, except with a Pivotal bent, of course.

THE REDMONK DISRUPTION

Just a few years into it, RedMonk decided to do away with their paywall and ended up showing one path to disrupting the industry analyst market: the idea of providing free analyst reports through blogs seemed crazy, but it worked. James captured the, uh, *esprit de corps* in the analyst world well in a 2005 post:

I was at a recent event when a well known industry analyst, who used to run a firm well known for writing white papers in support of vendor positions, sat down. I was discussing how blogs, RSS splicing and aggregation were going to change industry analyst and other information-based businesses. They sniffed and said that bloggers had no credibility. This from someone that sold their credibility down the river long ago.

Yup, analysts are a friendly lot...

As with VCs, one of the problems an analyst has is generating enough flow to get the raw materials you need for your day-to-day work: getting people to talk to you enough, frequently enough, and deeply enough to gather all the information you need to usefully pontificate. You need raw fodder for your content creation. Ben alludes to this is another way: you have to create a pipe (or an overflowing Evernote notebook) of content ideas, things to write and talk about...to analyze.

For RedMonk, having no paywall meant that their marketing was done for "free." The consequence was (and still is) that RedMonk can't charge for content, it's all free. Most firms in the industry analyst business charge *a lot* for content. My last analyst shop, 451 Research, charges a bundle, and people seem to like it: 451 writes great stuff and their large customer base shows that people value it. But, it does mean that 451 needs to do marketing separately; they don't get those "zero marketing budget" dynamics RedMonk does. Neither model is better or worse, just different depending on what and how you're running the business. Both models still get paid for consulting, webinars, and a multitude of other things.

Let's look at three firms to peek into the bushes of the business a little bit.

REDMONK'S DIFFERENTIATION

RedMonk thus differentiated itself from other analyst firms first by making all of its research free (at the time, very novel): it allowed RedMonk to build pull in the market, that is, it made marketing free. It wasn't easy, and it took awhile, but it worked.

Their research topics matched this structural approach as well, namely:

1. **focusing on bleeding edge technologies and practices, which, leads to the paid work on...**
2. **helping those bleeding edge companies talk to the "mainstream" IT world**
3. **helping "mainstream" IT vendors (IBM, Microsoft, Sun, Adobe, etc.) understand how to profit from and strategize/product plan with/around bleeding edge stuff.**

They still do that and do it well, along with some of the usual analyst business models (like consulting, webinars, events, etc.)...but all of RedMonk's activities revolve around knowing about the new shit sooner than the next analyst *and* being able to explain how to fit it into client thinking. Their events business (launched after I left) looks like an an adjacent business to the "knowing what the fuck we're talking about" strategy: the tried and true come "hang out with the smart folks and drink your face of" business model.

RedMonk is cheap compared to other firms. The entry level is $5,000 for startups, and goes up from there. Companies like IBM, SAP, and Microsoft pay a lot more (and get a lot more!) but still get a really good deal compared to what other firms charge. You can check out their client logo page to estimate their revenue if you do a little estimating for the larger account sizes and Excel swagging: not too shabby, eh?

THE 451 DIFFERENTIATION

451, structurally, is similar to other analyst outfits: there's a paywall for most everything. As with any analyst outfit, 451 does paid consulting, webinars, events, and other usual marketing driven stuff. 451 also does data center planning (they acquired The Uptime Institute some time ago) and has some interesting data-driven businesses that are being marshaled into proper quantitative analyst products. 451's key differentiation is mixing its scale with the "the new shit" focus (perhaps a bit less bleeding edge than RedMonk, but not much), all stuck in the speed blender of publishing velocity.

451 seeks out new technologies, not old ones, and writes a lot: each analyst has to write somewhere between 40–60 reports a year, basically one ~1,500 word report a week...not including other deliverables. For the most part, if you brief a 451 analyst they'll write a report on you, vendors love that and it helps with content flow (and gives analysts inbox heart-burn). I was terrible at that cadence coming from the RedMonk school (which emphasizes consulting, which I did a lot of at 451 instead of writing), but the best performers at 451 rarely take a briefing that resulting in no report being written.

451 is slightly cheaper than larger folks like Gartner and much more expensive than RedMonk. I was delightfully shocked at how much 451 charged coming from RedMonk; which is more a reflection of how

cheap RedMonk is (I'm not sure they've raised prices, at least at the entry level, since 2006 when I started there – great for clients!). You get a lot more content, of all types, however, from 451 than from RedMonk due to 451's sheer analyst bulk and core process of weekly report writing.

You'll recall that my personal revenue was much higher at 451. I think that's a reflection of the "leverage" a larger group of analysts can have: selling the same thing (reports and knowledge) over and over more.

GARTNER DIFFERENTIATION

Gartner is giant. It has breadth and has captured much marketshare. In analyst sales calls you often hear a variation on this:

Well, we're signing up with Gartner because we have to, and IDC next because we need their PivotTables… the rest of you get to fight over what's left (want to write a white paper for me?).

Gartner is really good at being the Microsoft of the analyst space…and I mean that as a compliment.

One of the key activities they do is ranking vendors. That may seem trivial, but it's huge. Gartner tells you what the safe bet in IT acquisition is. It may not be the growth bet, or even the anti-disruption bet for your industry, but it's the safe bet. And really, with the way most people use IT, that's all they want. People don't want to be Uber, they're

forced to compete with Uber, and they'd rather Uber didn't exist at all.

If this beguiles you, think about your own buying habits outside the realm of computers. Do you prefer to buy your building materials at Home Depot, or some experimental shop on the side of the road? Like lumber and Shop-Vacs, most people look to computers for a function, not a complex belief system (I could have typed "paradigm"), let alone putting a business strategy in action.

(We at Pivotal like to think we help companies who are wise enough to take the first mover advantage when it comes to using IT to gain competitive advantage. This is shockingly not everyone in the world, which is fine: so far there's been plenty of wise customers out there.)

Throw in their relative scale, and Gartner is in the hollowed "don't fuck it up" position.

Gartner is expensive, from what I've heard and encountered when I've been on the vendor side. However, depending on what you need their content is good and the ability to influence (that is, educate, not make them parrot your messaging) analysts through working with them is nice. The IIAR seems to like Gartner, that group of analyst relations folks having ranked Gartner as #1 most every year since 2008 (it's interesting to note that *individual* analyst winners are much different). Enterprises seem to like Gartner a lot as well from anecdotes I hear.

THE NEW "BLOGGERS-CUM-ANALYSTS"

The new (or "new new," if you're RedMonk and crew) crop of analysts follows the "make all the good stuff free" rule of having no paywalls (though Ben Thompson is following a sort of open core model). And in making all that stuff free,

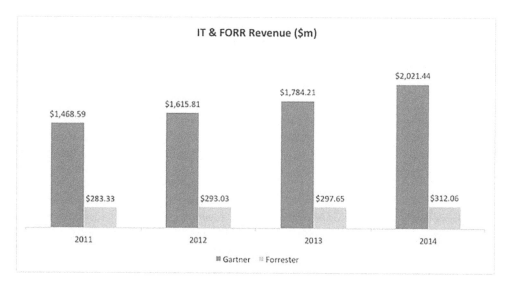

IT & FORR Revenue ($m)

2011 — $1,468.59 / $283.33
2012 — $1,615.81 / $293.03
2013 — $1,784.21 / $297.65
2014 — $2,021.44 / $312.06

Gartner   Forrester

they're doing much of the type of work that industry analysts do now, mostly of the qualitative sort. Horace gets into forecasts and market-sizing a bit, actually, which makes him even more of a threat; the other folks don't seem to spend time on that. (Of late Horace has been mixing in market numbers from traditional analyst shops as well, but he also doesn't do surveys.)

Again, the reason this new crop of "bloggers" are threatening to industry analysts is because they're serving some of the same purposes, with much of the same tools and outputs of traditional analysts. And for those analyst activities they don't currently do: it's not too far fetched to think that someone soon will. The core differences are similar to previous disruptors (RedMonk and 451 – see, that's why I outlined them above, all you tl;dr ding-a-lings!), but with some tweaks, namely:

NARROW FOCUS, BUT WITH BROAD APPEAL

Most of these analysts have a very narrow focus that appeals to a mainstream market. One individual can only cover so much, but if there's a large audience for that topic, it will suffice.

Horace ostensibly is the world's premier Apple analyst. That's a bold claim as I don't read any Apple analysts you have to pay to read, so maybe there's some better than him locked behind paywalls; at the very least, he's a big deal for his size. As a side effect of being an Apple analyst, he covers the mobile space in general. There's two more tricks for him that build off this seemingly narrow focus:

1. **In that smartphones and tablets are taking over how compute is done, he sort of covers "PCs of the future" and, thus, computers broadly.**

2. **"Innovation" is actually his main focus area, namely, figuring out what and how great companies actually do great things (as the intro to his podcast says, more or less). Apple is a wise choice for this question, but you can see his engineering-like "break it apart to find out how it works" curiosity at play when he looks at how Hollywood works (with Pixar as his Apple there), Amazon, and the mysteries of Google (cf. "The absence of a purpose rooted in profit makes Google resistant to analysis.").**

The combination of Apple, "PC of the future," and "innovation" all amounts to a very large "audience."

(Recently, Horace went to go work for a think-tank; it's hard to tell if that invalidates some of the "this independent blogger-cum-analyst thing is a thing" thinking here or not.)

While Ben Thompson started out *seemingly* as another Apple/mobile analyst, I'd argue he's become more of a "third platform" analyst, discussing how the "consumerization of IT," is effecting the tech industry.

THE EFFICIENCY OF VENDOR SPORTS

This narrow focus means that both (and most of these new types of analysts) cover "vendor sports": they don't give buyers advice about what products and services to buy, they instead tell you how various tech vendors are doing and explore the strategic possibilities of new types of technology.

There are very few of these new analysts that are prescriptive when it comes to buying. I'm not sure why, but I'd theorize that it has a lot to do with the cost structures of doing such work (in the cycle time of analysts learning, collecting epiphanies, publishing, and then collecting money form clients for sharing the results). This is a large part of why I think Gartner's scale and established position is and will continue to be hard to beat, head on at least.

There are some challengers here:

▸ I look towards folks like WiseGate, TrustRadius, Peerlyst, and even Spiceworks to sort out short-listing out.
▸ Folks over at places like The Virtualization Practice can help in their niche; if you wade through sites like BrainMadden.com you can get a sense of wise virtual desktop choices; and Horses for Sources seems like they'd be spot on for outsourcing short-listing.

Once these new bloggers move beyond vendor sports – if they can – and start recommending what to buy, the dynamics will change a lot. Until then, they're nibbling at the industry analyst business…but that's how it all starts.

BACK TO THE "ENTERPRISE GRUBER"

On that quest to find an enterprise Gruber, there's been a rash of sites of late that go for that. There's still a giant gap in the market for good enterprise tech coverage.

▸ TPM started up EnterpriseTech which seems to have taken the ethos of his wonderful IT Jungle (which seems to purposefully hide behind its ancient-feeling aesthetic – it's some of the best coverage and analysis of IBM that you'll find out there), and just announced a new site, The Platform.
▸ The Diginomica gang is having a run at enterprise applications.
▸ My friends at thenewstack.io are getting close and will soon give a view of how native advertising works the industry analyst business model blender.

I watch these sites closely to see how they pan out and if they fall into the usual journalistic traps that start to preclude good analysis.

HOW THE SMALL AND MID-SIZED FIRMS CAN REACT

What you'd really like to see is some dramatic business model hacking in the mid and small section of the industry analyst market. What would it mean to have a Ben Thompson or a RedMonk approach at a place like 451, or Forrester even? Those shops would have huge cultural issues to deal with (analysts are, ironically, a lot who're the least interested in doing new things in their own processes: they hate changing), but the established brand/reach and capital (in money *and* time) those larger firms could bring to the strategies of the micro firms would be interesting.

HOW THE BIG FIRMS CAN REACT

The problem with the big shops taking in the blogger-cum-analysts is that big shops don't like to create rock star analysts. The rock stars leave to become independent because they can make more money, or, at least have more freedom. They, like me, also get snatched up by vendors who can pay much more including something rarely seen in the analyst world: those mythical stock options which could worth anything between the title for a large house, the cost of a college diploma, or pack of novelty cup-cake papers.

Larger firms are better positioned to cement their position by upping their game by deeply evaluating and short-listing technologies. There are two examples right in front of us: OpenStack and Docker. Both of those vacillate between IaaS utopia (sometimes people come down from their buzz and realize that Docker often aspires to be a PaaS too) and shit-shows cracking in tire-fires all the way down.

Someone like a Gartner has the time, money, and (potential) authority to run labs to test technologies like these out and give solid recommendations on what to use and not use…per business use case, even. To quote the meme, one does not simply build an enterprise cloud…so how could you expect anyone who just creates PDFs about cloud to actually be credible?

SO, WHAT'S *YOUR* PROBLEM, COTÉ?

With all this glee, you may be wondering why I'm now at a vendor. Good question, as they say when they're buying time to think. The core of it is that my fixed expenses are too high. I have a family, a large house, and even a new dog (I resisted as long as I could – promise!). And, I'm the single earner for all that.

While I would love to bushwhack my way through this emerging analyst jungle, I don't want to *Mosquito Coast* my family; and let's be honest, myself either. The warm, bi-weekly embrace of a vendor is very comforting. So, like the analysts themselves who observe from the sideline, I'll be eagerly watching how the industry analyst sports-ball brackets play out.

AR pros are not scheduling coordinators

Suyog Shetty

he technology services industry has evolved at such a frightful pace in recent months, I won't be surprised that in some time it may be renamed as Digital Services industry doing completely away with the traditional era terms. In the immediate future, some of the older legacy phrases may just fade away too and if you happen to accidentally glance your archived notes and stumble on words like ERP, PCs, TCP – you may wonder just how we managed them all.

Many of us in marketing or allied areas probably took a cursory glance at several of such technology deployments, and understood them at a superficial level. From thereon, had a quick glance of some of the 'decks', added some dollops of prose and there is your pitch. Several times without even collaborating with the technology experts. A quick snip, snap job. Precisely for this reason the inability to convincingly narrate, articulate and comprehend how technology specifically solves business and functional issues became the sore

point for some leaders. This gradual build-up of a shallow knowledge base resulted in several leaders believing that Analyst Relations professionals are just 'meeting schedulers'.

At times, without setting expectations it is expected that the content is like any other pitch. It's a simple job of getting the jargon in place, leverage the software package for some glossy icons, charts, throw in that abused image of a cloud and there you are, the deck sitting pretty ready to be relayed! Familiar – isn't it? Imagine, receiving this every hour, every day from all kinds of enterprises.

When does it Begin?

The entire process commences much before you even reach out to the research firm. It's the introspection you do after understanding what an organization is aiming to be best at. Not just revenue, headcount numbers, but the ability to construct the story line on what are we taking, for whom, and how that will accelerate them (the customer) to grow much, much faster. For instance, create a war room when preparing for the marquee ranking reports and allocate roles to multiple folks. Set expectations, brief, get them to deliver, evaluate.

Once you have the draft ready, request another analyst (of the same firm) to give you an audience for a rehearsal before you finally go on air for that final pitch of the Wave or MQ or MarketScape. The feedback, critique you'd receive will be enormous, and the perspectives provided will add tremendously to your final product that will get presented to that end customer (the analysts).

Remember, it's a story not just to be narrated, but the ability to enable the listener to Experience it. And the prep to that Experience takes weeks, months to hone. Daunting, but worth every second you spend.

Effort-less

The efforts required are massive, but these practices can be replicated and improved after several levels of engagements. Very often, it is mistaken to be the next level of Public Relations and by that I don't demean what PR professionals do. The essence for AR teams is to be able to deliver the pitch if the respective leader is not available. This is easier said than done, as several times the content is extremely technical and does need a seasoned hand to deliver the message effectively. However, if the storyline is strong enough to convince the analyst – AR professionals too should be able to understand and simplify the conversation discussion. Don't we all love sessions that simplify how hybrid cloud gives superior benefits to a customer who is unable to decide between a public and private one!

At every given opportunity if AR professionals step up to volunteer and deliver what businesses do, the perspective of technology leaders improves dramatically. The takeaway for them is – here is a team that not only has superlative analyst relationships, but also knows how to walk the talk, how to pitch, respond to queries convincingly, and summarize succinctly. A strong reinforcement where the AR teams can get involved in several nuances as the business team devise plans for their customer engagement requirements.

Internal drill

The fundamental steps commence when the AR leader acknowledges the need, as well as ensures the team members undergo a series of prep sessions. A genuine effort requires time, investments, and series of consistent feedback sessions that will change the approach to the entire lifecycle. Some of the top analysts too can help provide you feedback on your thought process and areas to improve. Additionally, several marketing

team members already have immense exposure to various horizontal and verticals through their day to day engagements, and that can be effectively used as well. With immense potential available that needs to be harnessed, the ability to carefully nurture skill sets in best possible manner will remain critical.

With Digital now becoming the signpost of success, AR professionals are today in an exciting period by being able to introduce an ingenious approach using various tenets through mobile devices, twitter handles, LinkedIn updates and so on.

We are now at the cusp of changing the game, in a way and approach we want to. Let's go grab it!

Can Legacy Analysts Survive?
The Proof of the Pudding is in the Eating

ndustry analysts don't need to have more industry experience than their clients – any more than accountants, management consultants or any other professionals – in order to add value. James Gardner and David Rossiter, who recently criticised analyst firms along these lines, ignore the glaring reality that analysts firms have continued to perform well. That suggests that their core business model isn't broken, and that unexplored opportunities remain minimal.

Gardner argues that analysts are glorified journalists. Their reports are based on interviews with business people, but they don't have the expertise of their clients.

"It always reminds me of the proverbial food critic. They can eat what the chef prepares and pass judgement, but don't put them in a kitchen if what you want is something edible. There is value in the opinion, of course, but the point is the food."

James has a second concern, that some analyst firms sell seats, rather than all-you-can eat enterprise pricing.

"They send their account managers in to visit with people who are not named seat holders, and start to sell them the benefits of having access to the research. Then, of course, we get a call from these individuals asking for access. It puts us in the invidious position of having to tell people that their needs are less important than those of others. We have a fixed budget for analyst research, not one that can flex upwards because it is convenient for the account manager."

James mellows a little, saying that "there is some value in analyst research, and that the reports written by the superstars have a value that counteracts the journalistic reporting" … "But we need to be able to use that insight broadly in our business. And we don't want named seats. It's too hard to make it work. We also don't want an "enterprise" licence, which amounts to buying a named seat for everyone." His message to the top analyst firms he currently uses is: "your time with us is limited if you don't make it easy for us to get value from what we buy. "

James doesn't have the budget to give access to everyone who wants it. He'd like to give everyone access, without having to pay extra. If he can't get more, then he'll go elsewhere.

James' fundamental complaint is not about the quality of analysis, but about the pricing model in which you get more as you pay more. That is, of course, pretty much the dominant pricing model for everything. David picks up James' complaints about quality, and runs with them:

I spend a large portion of my life educating people about the value of the industry analysts.

Then you set up a meeting – either a briefing or an inquiry call – and in strolls someone who knows less about the market than I do (never mind my CEO, CMO, product manager or technology guru). It is happening more and more frequently. It's almost as if the industry analyst firms have a death wish.

Get wise guys. People pay a lot of money for your insight. You're important because of your influence. You're valuable because you're the experts.

James and David seem to rest their views on assumptions which, as far as we can see, are mistake. This is how we see it:

Most analysts don't need their clients' technical expertise to be effective. Food critics need to be good journalists more than they need to be good cooks, because writing is the core task. Critics don't need to cook at all, and analysts don't need to code. It's nice but, for most clients, not necessary. Analysts add value by offering insight that the client does not, and cannot develop easily, in the context of a single firm.

It's a fantasy to think that analysts, who generally tend to focus on technologies in their growth phase, will either have the expertise of the people they meet, or will care to show that they do. It's not necessary, but it's also just not possible. It's an unreasonable expectation to think that analysts who have to work across several technologies during their research career will be at the leading edge of any of them by the time they meet the client. Folk need to understand that that the reality of the analyst industry is that staff with different levels of expertise will be there in client-facing roles, as is the case with other professional services firms. There are veterans, there are experienced professionals new to a particular segment, and there will be entry-level staff.

Indeed, the fact that many analysts lack the client's deep domain expertise is sometimes an advantage to analyst relations professionals and to clients. AR professionals have the opportunity to help develop fresh analysts understanding of the market, in a way they cannot do with industry veterans. And they bring fresh ideas and outside information.

Were this not the fact, then how could we otherwise explain the ability of top analyst firms to survive and flourish? As with other management consultancies, clients understand that the large analyst firms are more than the sum of their parts. They have not only individuals with serious professional backgrounds, but also unrivaled access into the whole IT supply chain and huge analytic and research resources.

All professional services firms have detractors among their clients: everyone likes to complain about consultants, accountants and other advisers. However the reality is that those firms have solid client retention rates and face no serious threat of losing their most valuable clients.

Market analysts are people in a continual process of remaking themselves as experts, because areas and technologies continually change. Both the research process and the client service process are aspects of refining their expertise. Both AR professionals and analyst clients have to realise that there is value in analysts, even if they are working as hard as you are to understand the markets.

Of course James does understand that: it's just that he wants to get enterprise-wide access to the top analyst firms for the same price as limited seats. The reason why he cannot is a simple matter of market forces. By moving from community pricing to individual seats, the top analyst firms have doubled their revenue per seat without any substantial erosion in client numbers. Almost all that extra revenue goes straight to the bottom line. They would give that up, for no corresponding gain, by reversing direction. One might as well ask Microsoft or Apple to stop selling product by the unit.

What would happen, of course, if the analyst firms tried to follow this guidance? If they replaced all their staff with industry veterans, and then gave enterprise-wide access for the same cost as their current contracts? They would simultaneously increase costs and decrease revenues. That would be a lose-lose solution – the firms would go bust, and the clients would lose their guidance.

There are – certainly -many reasons to criticise analyst firms. However, there are 900 analyst firms. Most of them are tiny businesses run by experts that struggle to deliver the same value as larger firms – if they did, then they would make more revenue per employee. You don't need to be a chef to know that the proof of the pudding is in the eating.

Like it or not, the analysts' business model is not broken.

If the business model was broken then top analyst firms like Gartner and Forrester would underperform their competitors: that's the key point underpinning our recent defence of analysts. In fact, the top firms are increasing their lead. Their approach is producing unhappy customers but any resulting loss in customers is much smaller than the corresponding revenue increases that result from seat-based pricing.

Don't misunderstand the motivation for these comments: The analyst firms are not my clients. I'm a former analyst, and our firm tracks the analyst industry for clients in the high-technology and telecoms markets. I think it's important that analyst

firms' clients take a realistic view at the value those firms provide, as many folk are doing. There's no point, to take one common example, complaining to analysts when their industry forecasts don't get within 5% of the actual number: market forces just don't support much greater accuracy than we have now. People need to understand what they will get from analysts, and look elsewhere if they need something else.

In the IT services space, in particular, we have seen the growth of third party advisory firms whose consultants are, overwhelmingly, industry veterans. They advise on procurement and their advisors' skill is really more on negotiation rather than on research. But there can be a downside to using consultants whose expertise comes from past experience rather than current research (and, generally, folk at those advisory firms are not centred around ongoing research projects). They tend to base their guidance on their own experience, which means they tend to offer technical guidance based on solutions which have crossed the chasm into mass adoption (Of course you could hire Tom DeMarco or Tim Lister, but their hourly rates and availability might limit your access).

The challenge to any alternative business model is how to monetise the value created by providing research to clients at a lower price point. There are two principal alternatives:

1. **Fake open source (vendor-funded research given away, not produce using an open source approach), in which extra value is generated for the vendor who therefore pays (Read the debate on my article 'Is free analyst research really "open source"?' at influencerrelations. com/808).**

2. **Leave money on the table (strip down costs through lower remuneration,**

iterative and incremental development of ideas, and the reuse of ideas from the vendor and user communities), in which talented analysts like James Governor forego the benefits they might experience in larger firms in order to test out a different business model.

Such approaches produce different outputs from the top analyst firms, as would the highly marginal third option: real open source of the type aimed for by Wikibon. All of these approaches tend to use less systematic interviewing of mainstream users outside the blogosphere, because of the high cost of basic research.

Of course, there are other alternatives to paying by the seat. Many clients fear pay-per-view pricing because of the uncertain upper value of the service.

The business model used by the top analyst firms disappoints and frustrates some clients, a few of whom will take some of their money elsewhere. But, as long as the top analyst firms continue to outperform their peers, we can't say their business model is broken. Demand for their work is relatively price-inelastic, and that is not likely to change.

Thought Leaders

Thought leaders are characterised by thinking differently about important issues. Martin Luther King was a thought leader – his vision of a society where whites and blacks could live together changed the rules of thinking and behaviour in American society. The British nurse Florence Nightingale was a thought leader. She changed the 19th-century philosophy in health care, amongst others through the promotion of the importance of hygiene. Steve Jobs was hailed as a thought leader. He changed the way we look at the use of computer technology. These three persons contributed to this world with their vision and indeed, were eventually seen as thought leaders. But what is thought leadership in an organisational context? Why should organisations want to promote thought leadership?

And how do you build this? How many thought leaders do you know personally?

Since we can't all be thought leaders, you need to make sure this will not be another overrated phrase used in today's media. We should keep some things off the radar and only come out with those when they really have a meaning. Today I decided to check my LinkedIn connections. Forty people have the phrase "thought leader" in their profile. Some even have it with their specialties. You've got to love that. Please explain to me how someone is an account manager, but on the side a thought leader as well. What qualifies you as a thought leader, if you have been selling software for the past ten years? I then decided to look up some people I greatly admire, and whom I consider qualified to be a thought leader. It turns out that they hardly use this phrase, and each of them contributed greatly to the world of business today. So should you come up with it yourself or should you wait until people start calling you a thought leader?

In the space of Influencer Relations there are many people who think they have it all figured out, but I guess it is not so different in other sectors. I just want to make people aware of the fact that putting something on your resume, doesn't automatically make it true. This works both ways of course. Why do people have such an issue with acknowledging their peers? Does that make you a lesser person in that field? I doubt it. I really think it shows that you are open for other people to be recognised for their efforts. But at the very least let us all agree that the phrase "thought leader" is not the new "Manager" or "Consultant". That would do so many great people injustice.

Your pitch to analysts isn't just about your solution

*I*n pitches to analysts, there are many conversations going on. At one level, there's a communication about the business solution. There's also a conversation about the wider market and about the personal credibility of the participants. Sometimes the slides used in pitches are just excuses for the interaction. The slides are used to assess both the market vision of the firm and the adaptability if the executives to adjust to the market and conversation. The solution pitch is used to assess the ability of executives to adapt.

In the body of theory used by business sociologists, we talk about inscription devices. Pitch slides provide, in the same way as analyst research,

both a vision to be signed up to and also an entry ticket into a conversation. In our 2014 survey, we saw that pitch decks (which play similar roles to business plans in entrepreneurial pitches to investors, in explaining the business) were important. We expected people to respond to our survey by stressing the vision in the pitch decks. As the chart below shows, many analysts found that a valuable part of pitches was the broader discussion about market categories and trends. However, we were surprised to see how important presentational elements, such personal credibility and value, mattered. So, looking at the non-PowerPoint content of a pitch to analysts allows us to see other, perhaps intrinsic, qualities of valuable professionals who interact in pitches to analysts. In the pitch to analysts, of course, analysts are not prospective customers looking to buy the solution.

Both the analysts and the vendors produce artefacts that outline the vision of the market, and what it means for them, that they want the ecosystem to perform. Analysts' research is as much a pitch as the patter of a street-trader. Market traders are providing both goods to customers, and valuable social interactions that give knowledge, entertainment, connections, status and potential access to other resources. The intrinsic object is often not the main value. When an analyst is being pitched to they are not getting a valuable product; they are exchanging information that allows both sides to produce more successfully performative visions of the future. It's not only the knowledge of the market that is exchanged. There is a lot of name-dropping, status-building, praise and similar methods that aim to build personal rapport.

I've seen this first hand watching firms of different size in the same market who are pitching to the same analyst for the same study. Larger firms get an easy ride in some ways: the functionality and suitability of their solutions are less likely to be challenged. It's easy to see why if you see how that would work in a consumer market. Certainly, analysts have to value the product or service delivery of a firm. But the range of artefacts like the Magic Quadrant shows that there's multiple things being evaluated at any one time. Not only the intrinsic quality of the solution's execution but also the ability of the firm to use organising visions of the future to create, explain, adapt and convince. Both the concrete and the socially-formed are the multiple levels of the valuation process. Their interplay continually reforms the different criteria being valued in pitched to analysts. Furthermore, while analysts are valuing providers through their pitches it's also the case that the providers are also valuing the analysts.

When vendors come to pitch, there are three levels therefore.

In practice, which of these factors are most important for a successful pitch to another person?
[Ratio: Industry Analyst/Investor] n=63
Source: influencerrelations.com/3348

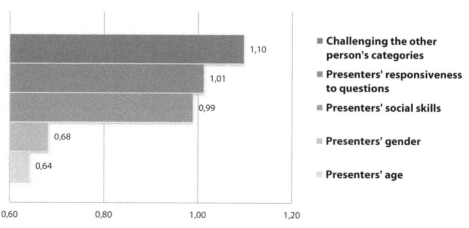

1. **About the products**
2. **About markets and how the definition of market categories are defined and how they evolve**
3. **The value of the actors.**

So, different things are being valued at the same time. A managerial focus will always encourage vendors to place too much emphasis on the solution, and less on the struggle to change valuation criteria. However, it's often ignored that people are being valued, and organisations are being valued by analysts though their selection of people. We saw this in our 2014 study. When analysts are sent both slides and biographies in advance, then often it's the biographies that are being examined most closely. Analysts know about the tangible aspects of their markets; they need to know about the future and to be able to evaluate the credibility of the people they are being pitched to by.

These aspects of personal credibility have to be contextualised. The work of assessing products and markets is real and important in, and after, pitches. But that's clearly not the only thing going on. By shining a light on the impressions that people leave on each other, and how they are valued we don't want to suggest that analysts are being led only by flim-flam. But it is useful to explore what is not explained by traditional narratives of pitches, which focus only on the solutions that are under discussion. My academic colleague Christian Hampel and I explored this, aiming to show that there is another conversation at work. We used the work of Erwin Goffman to try to understand the role of presentation. His approach is valuable, even if there are many criticisms of it and attempts ti build on his approach. Goffman's work didn't focus on very similar interactions. Much of his work, for example, was done in hotel restaurants and cafes. Unlike a waiter and a customer meeting in a cafe, both sides in a pitch to analysts bring a menu and both are trying to prove themselves through a discussion about the non-immediate future. If IBM promises a smart city, that's not like promising a burger with fries. Analysts assume more power in a pitch than either waiters or customers in cafes. Coaching can flow both ways, even unsolicited, as vendors try to increase the favourability of analysts and to increase the influence of favourable analysts.

Goffman's approach focusses on interactions that are physically co-located, and so a future concern for us could to understand the different impact if any of online interactions. So many pitches to analysts now happen online. Trevor Pinch, who has made a seminar study of pitches by street traders, was written a lot about the invisible technologies within the Goffman approach. John Law's work as also helped us to better understand pitches. Ruth Rettie's thoughts about online impression management have given us a lot of ideas, especially about the back-stage and on-stage elements of the drama being mobilised by these experts who gather in pitch meetings. When these solution providers are 'on stage' there are comparisons with dramaturgy that can give us some powerful, often analogous, insights.

Drive

How to measure analysts' and influence

A wake-up call for technology vendors: Don't wait for the aliens to land

*W*hen asked about analysts and analyst relations the reaction of technology vendors seems to be divided into two main groups. Those that believe that analyst relations is something a vendor is supposed to work on and those that believe that analysts are an external force – some kind of godlike alien species – that works in a complete vacuum and that will sometime in the future knock on their door to take them to a better planet (or alternatively blast them to hell by putting them in the bottom left corner of a market study).

My favorite quote from the second group – one which is actually a more common example of mindset than you would believe – is the following:

"Dear XXX, we currently do not have any budget for this kind of things. At the moment we do not care too much about analysts, once they can't ignore us they will write about us anyway. And influencing analysts is fooling yourself. Better to have clear results they can't deny, right?"

Now obviously this vendor is a strong believer in what in economics is called a "perfect market". This perfect market implies a 100% availability of all information for all market participants at all times. It also implies that there is no effort associated with gathering information and making sense of it. In reality however it is quite unlikely that an analyst will be able to find, interpret and analyse all the vendors and information that is available at any given time. So providing information for (or withholding it from) an analyst is a kind of influence that is quite real.

Relying on the analyst community to do all the work for you is a dangerous thing because in many cases there will be more than one vendor in any technology space that can solve a customer problem. Now if one thinks about it this isn't so different from what is happening all over the market. Every buyer tries to spot the perfect solution in the market by gathering information about what is available. Now I wonder if all the vendors that are subscribing to the earlier quote also agree that doing any marketing targeted at all those buyers out there is a waste of time because by some miraculous means they will be able to spot the perfect solution anyway.

Of course an analyst is supposed to have a more comprehensive understanding of a market and will probably spend more time analyzing what is available than an ordinary customer but then again he has to deal with a global market and he cannot narrow down the field by simply deciding that a number of features is not relevant for his specific use case. In addition most analysts are simply really busy people and it might not be a good idea to base your analyst relations strategy on the assumption that they will make the time available to notice you right at that moment when you happen to reach the pinnacle of your efforts.

Analyst Relations isn't about having one interaction at that one magic moment when the alien space ship comes to pick you up. It is more apt to think of it as a kind of SETI project where you listen for messages and where you help guide your alien visitors to a landing space right in your backyard. This process requires skill, dedication and patience and this is also why it is a profession and why there are professional service providers out there to help you. Now wouldn't it be cool to have "first contact"? Maybe once you start talking to them you will find out that they aren't so different after all.

The 5 I's of
Analyst Relations

n the bustle of daily activities, it is sometimes hard for Analyst Relations (AR) managers to keep their teams focused on their key operational activities. Kea Company created the 5 I's of Analyst Relations to provide an easy mantra of essential activities.

The 5 I's are:

▸ Identify (The Most Influential Analysts)
  > Ranked and tiered analyst list(s)
  > Continuous research on the analysts' coverage
▸ Interact (In the Correct Ways)
  > Mix of one-to-one, one-to-many, none-to-many types
  > Mix of briefings, SAS, relationship meetings and client inquiries
▸ Information (Most Appropriate in Correct Context)
  > Analyst needs are different from sales, press and investors
  > Supports three forms of analyst research delivery
▸ Improve (The Relationship Continuously)
  > Become part of the analysts' informal research network
  > Achieve strategic connection with the top Tier One analysts
▸ Infrastructure (The Right Tools and Processes)
  > Organisation, processes, management and staffing
  > Portals and ARM-analyst relationship management application

Obviously, getting up every morning and chanting "Identify, Interact, Information, Improve, Infrastructure" ten times will not ensure a smooth operating AR function. However, thinking about these 5 I's in key situations will improve your efficiency and effectiveness.

An example – An AR professional gets a call from an unknown analyst at an unknown firm asking for information and a briefing. AR's normal customer centric approach, reinforced by being too busy to think, would be to agree to the briefing. However, if the AR professional is operating by "Identify – the Most Influential Analysts" they would likely say "Sorry, can't help". This is because it is unlikely that a relevant and influential analyst would be totally unknown to them. At a minimum, the AR professional would at least investigate the relevance of the analyst before committing to spending precious AR bandwidth and executive time agreeing to respond.

By maintaining a ranked and tiered list of the key influencers in their market an AR team can quickly determine how to react to analyst requests. This allows them to allocate their time and political capital with executives to the analysts that matter.

Bottom Line: Because AR is very interrupt driven it is useful to have an operational framework that makes it easy to keep focused on key priorities. The 5 I's of AR is a straightforward set of operating principles that AR teams should adopt.

Getting started
with
Analyst Relations:
In-house or
external AR
agency?

*G*etting started with analyst relations can prove to be quite a challenge if a company does not have any previous experience in dealing with analyst companies. At this point it is time to consider the alternatives of in-house analyst relations and/or utilizing an external analyst relations agency.

From the perspective of the corporation, it seems obvious that the company can represent itself better than any agency. However, much of what an agency does isn't representation. Organizing and planning the analyst relations strategy, coaching internal AR stakeholders and measuring the AR success also falls into the realm of an AR agency. On the other hand it can sometimes be tough for an outside agency to get access to the contact person or information needed to brief or update an analyst. Also an analyst may prefer dealing with senior company representatives directly because they might feel that this will give them easier access to internal information not readily available outside the company.

I have been in both positions and my experience is that there are a number of benefits in utilising a specialised analyst relations agency. The major difference will always be that in house teams have experience of one vendor, whereas

agencies can implement the best practices and lessons learned from many interactions. Also they probably already know many of the analysts a company wants to reach and understand the internal workings of the various analyst firms. In addition there is an advantage in an objective 3rd party view. Too much elation for the own company and its products might not be received well by the analysts since it can be seen as a lack of perspective/insight on the companies real position in the market.

Having worked with many vendors throughout my time at Gartner I have seen some good and quite a few bad examples for both options. I work for a consultancy now with clients who are more than happy with the support they get for analyst relations and influencer marketing. It is my opinion that in the end the right decision depends on the available resources (time, money and expertise) a company can "spare" for analyst relations. For many emerging and mid-size vendors it will be hard to allocate the necessary (full-time) resources for an efficient analyst relations approach. In these cases it makes perfect sense to leverage the expertise an analyst relations agency can provide to avoid mistakes and ensure professional planning and execution of the analyst relations activities.

CONFIDENTIAL

Don't Panic if your Competitor Hires Your Gartner Analyst

*G*artner's French Caldwell retired last month; this week he joins MetricStream, one of the GRC vendors he followed for Gartner. Folk are often surprised when top analysts move over to the supplier side. Howard Dresner, one of the best known analysts in any field, surprised a lot of people when he left Gartner to join Hyperion. While it's only human to be worried, there's no cause for panic. Former META Group SVP Christian Byrnes (@cbyrnes), now Managing Vice President at Gartner, said in an email to me and my peers:

Every employee of Gartner is subject to our Confidentiality Agreement. And, in the case of analysts, we are very aware of the trust given to us by vendor clients during inquiries, SAS and briefings. As such, analysts are trained in the proper handling of such information. When an analyst leaves Gartner, they are reminded of that fact and they must acknowledge that they understand that their responsibility concerning confidentiality goes with them. This even includes when analysts retire. I realize that this is a very sensitive issue for any client who has entrusted Gartner with its strategic plans. You should know that this is something that we take very seriously at the highest levels of the company.

Analysts often cross over onto the vendor side, especially because firms like Gartner are enthusiastic about non-competitive clauses in its employment contracts. They prevent employees from continuing to work as an analyst for a period if they leave Gartner. Someone like Richard Stiennon, formerly a top Gartner security analyst, for example, is possibly worth more to another analyst firm than to a vendor. However, he could only take employment on the vendor side for a certain period of time.

But this forces Gartner's analysts into a difficult position: to leave ethically, how can they start flagging up to their clients and colleagues that they intend to leave, without the risk that some vendors will stop talking to them, and thus make it impossible to work during their notice period?

What Gartner does, where possible, is to start that process several months in advance. In Dresner's case they were able to tell people about the intended move. Several months is a long time, during which things could change a lot, either in an analyst house, in a vendor, or in an analyst's life. Both the analyst and the analyst house have to accept a substantial downside in the analyst's ability to gather knowledge and advise clients during that period if they announce where the analyst is going. The alternative is to restructure the research without flagging up the analyst's departure, but using the restructure as a way of bothering the information that the outgoing analyst has in a more systematic way. Although it did not know Caldwell's plans, Gartner started that process in February, by announcing a total overhaul of GRC coverage project managed by Candace Hugdahl. It replaced Caldwell's MQ with other reports delivered by a team of analysts. That allowed vendors to get weaned off French, and comfortable with the new team.

Clearly, from Gartner's point of view, the down-side of reorganisation and the calls from anxious clients that Candace might be getting today are not only in their clients' objective interests, but are also worth much less than the risk of allowing its competitors to offer a home to analysts who want to move on and up in the analyst industry.

Why Have An Analyst / Consultant Relations Programme?

For two reasons:
1. To save money.
2. To get better results.

Your firm will save money because it costs less to do any job when it's done by people who know how to do it and are motivated to do it well. This reflects economies of scale (the more of something you do, the less each unit costs) and the learning curve (the more of something you've done, the less the next unit costs). Your firm will get better results because people who are hired to

do a job do it better than people who have it tacked onto their other responsibilities.

The Analyst/Consultant Relations Idea

Part of what analysts and consultants think about you is objective. You either do or don't have a router with eight ports, an office in India, or the ability to import .xlsx files. Analyst or consultant support cannot affect any of those. If an analyst or consultant mentions anything in this category, the facts will determine what he or she says. The rest is subjective. Will your firm stay current with technology? Is its strategic direction aligned with industry trends? Is your support up to par? There are no objective measures for any of these, yet they are important to any recommendation.

Your analyst/consultant relations program is not their only source of information on these. Take support. Analysts will ask your customers about your support. That, however, is second-hand information. Their only direct information about your support comes from how well you support them.

The IDEAL Framework

Every part of an analyst/consultant relations program fits one of the five IDEAL categories:
▸ **I**dentify
▸ **D**rive
▸ **E**xecute
▸ **A**lign
▸ **L**everage

Identify refers to identifying your analyst/consultant relations targets. As a category of activity, it also includes planning the program: identifying what needs to be done. Drive refers to putting programs in place that will drive operational excellence.

Execute is carrying out the program activities, engaging with analysts and consultants. Align means aligning what you do with corporate messages and strategies. Leverage is taking advantage of analyst/consultant relations to bring value to your company, leveraging your relationships for strategic benefit. That makes your program a strategic adjunct to business development. That is your goal.

A Bit of Perspective on How Analysts and Consultants Influence Sales

Every purchase has a decision maker, a person who says "we'll buy this" or "we'll buy that" with no fear of being overridden. This person can always be identified. The decision maker must be sold on the product or service. Even when the bulk of selling time is spent with other people, usually those who make recommendations to this person, it is ultimately necessary to make sure that he or she is convinced as well.

Analyst/consultant relations are not the only factor in sales success. Companies with top-notch products in growing markets can succeed despite poor analyst/consultant relations. Companies with excellent analyst/consultant relations, conversely, can fail if they don't execute in product planning or development. If a company's R&D is behind the times, its products cost more than they should, or its customer support is inadequate, no analyst or consultant relations program can compensate. Management must understand this. Miracles should not be part of the analyst/consultant relations job description. A new analyst or consultant relations program is also not a quick fix for years of neglect. It won't make a difference overnight. It's like losing weight: ten years' gain won't come off in a week.

Analyst/consultant relations are, however, part of the picture. If they are done well and continued they can make a good company even more successful, help any company weather hard times, and in borderline situations make the difference between survival and bankruptcy.

By analogy: a boxer with one hand tied behind his back can win if he is sufficiently larger, stronger or more skilled than his opponent. Despite this, boxers don't enter the ring with one hand tied behind their backs. They can't afford to concede any advantage. So it is with analyst and consultant relations. They are a competitive weapon. No information technology firm can afford to give them up.

Analyst Relations – Nothing Start-ups Should Worry About. Or Should They?

*I*t is a common belief that the playing field of analyst relations is reserved for the 'big guys' who are spending lots of money on their relationship with the analyst companies. And for the most part it is true that it is mostly established companies that have implemented structured analyst relations programs. For this reason it obviously is a waste of time and resources for any emerging vendor to engage in this discipline – for how should he ever be able to compete with the established companies, right? Certainly the analysts will always spend a considerable amount of time covering the established players in the market but it is equally important for the analysts to be aware of what is happening in the market and what new trends and technologies are gaining ground. More often than not it is start-ups that dare to do things differently and help to establish a new trend. Of course you can wait until your technology has reached maturity and has become mainstream before getting in touch with analysts, but by acting this way start-ups are missing out on the chances offered by efficient analyst relations activities.

As with anything else analyst relations involve a learning curve and it takes (a lot of) time to establish working relationships with analysts. This reason alone should be enough for start-ups to start with analyst relations as early as possible. Starting an analyst relations program from scratch later on when a company realises that it desperately needs to get on the radar screen of the analysts (be it to get some traction with large enterprise customers, venture capitals or technology / channel partners) will not only be much more expensive but it will in all likelihood not work at all. Without laying the groundwork and without a history of engaging with the analysts it will be very tough to ramp up a successful analyst relations program on short notice.

Besides the time factor there are several benefits in being a small vendor when engaging with the analysts. For example there are some analyst publications (e. g. Cool Vendor reports) that are 'reserved' for covering small vendors with unique technologies or business models. Also the analysts will be eager to hear about new technologies and solutions if they align with their research agenda or with a perceived end-user demand in the market.

Tailoring your message to address these analyst needs is one of the core challenges faced by small vendors. By talking to the analysts and reading their published research small vendors will be able to get a valuable 3rd party perspective on the market, their technology and their G2M strategy. This will also give the vendor a better understanding of the focus areas of the various analysts which in turn will help to fine tune the analyst relations activities and the corporate messaging. In addition to this even small pieces of advice given by an analyst in the early phases of a start-up may be critical to their success later on.

Considering that start-ups only have a limited window to establish themselves in the market and usually lack the time and resources to run extensive push marketing campaigns it is imperative that they leverage the potential represented by analyst relations. Being noticed and mentioned by analyst companies will help them establish the market reach and credibility they need to succeed in the market.

Analyst Relations Programs: The Top 5 Biggest Mistakes

5. Vendors approach analysts with an undifferentiated message and lack of thought in their vision and strategy.

Downside – why should an analyst pay any attention to a boring, me too vendor, especially if the market is crowded and fragmented?

4. Vendors provide the wrong type of information, not supporting the methods the analysts use to communicate with end users. This problem is especially common with product companies run by engineers who are totally in love with the features and functions of their products. These vendors only want to talk speeds-and-feeds and ignore the more important types of information that analysts need.

Downside–vendors can miss impacting an analyst's verbal communication in a client one-on-one by providing only the facts and figures used in written research.

3. Vendors use the same approach used for all analysts and all firms. Some firms have very bureaucratic briefing request procedures while others permit vendors and PR firms to call the analysts directly. Market researchers need numbers while advisory analysts provide customer success stories. Some analysts are very structured in the information they want and the briefing structure while other analysts even at the same firm are very informal.

Downside – analysts are narcissistic prima donnas who want to do things their way. Vendors who ignore basic differences between analysts and firms run the risk of irritating the analysts, not providing needed information and wasting the analysts' time.

2. Vendors obsess with conducting face-to-face formal meetings instead of using a mix of interaction types. The analyst roadshow is the most expensive interaction in terms of time and money and the most difficult way to interact with analysts.

Downside – AR programs miss the opportunity to interact more effectively with analysts by ignoring other interaction avenues like the phone, e-mail, teleconferences, webinars and summits.

1. Vendors mis-use their analyst briefing lists. AR programs target the wrong analysts because:
▸ They don't have analysts with the right coverage on their lists
▸ They talk to analysts with business models that do not fit their AR or corporate objectives
▸ They have too few or too many analysts on their lists
▸ They do not rank and tier their analysts so they can concentrate on the most important tier 1 analysts
▸ They have a one-size fits all list instead of breaking it out by product lines

Downside – Talking to the wrong analysts is a waste of time with the huge opportunity cost of missing the analysts who could actually impact your company.

Bottom Line: Many AR programs suffer the same mishaps regardless of the company type: software, hardware, services or Internet companies. AR staffs need to look seriously at their programs to see if they fall prey to these mistakes. Then they need to ruthlessly root out the practices that lead to these mistakes.

Influencer Relations Do's and Don'ts: Have You Read Something Boring Today?

I bet you have – but since it was so boring you probably cannot remember what it was. Now turn the question around and ask yourself what you have written (or said) today that might have been pretty boring for someone else?

Within influencer marketing not being boring is one of the key challenges. Influencers (e. g. industry analysts, editors or bloggers) are always keen to stay ahead in their respective fields. This means that the most likely way to catch their attention is by providing information that has not been beaten to death everywhere else before. The problem is figuring out what is truly unique about your company and/or your solution. It is quite easy to get blinded by routine when working for a single company. You are probably keeping track of a number of obvious competitors and some publications relevant for your area of expertise but do you truly know what is happening outside your own backyard? Chances are that someone – e. g. an industry analyst who has spent a number of years screening vendors and looking for (and shaping) new trends – has come across the same ideas before. For this reason it makes sense to take a close look at what

the influencers you are about to engage with are currently focusing on and what they have covered in the past. Besides spending some time with research it might make sense to double-check your pitch with experts outside your company who have some experience in dealing with the influencers you are about to engage with. This will not only help you to avoid featuring something as 'unique' that has already been covered in writing by the influencer in question but will also give you the chance to focus on areas of interest of the influencer thus increasing the chances of getting some coverage and mind share.

Another point to remember is that influencers are looking for deep insights into their topics. Sure, it might take some courage to share your vision and road-map with someone outside your company but taking this chance might be the key to establishing a trusted relationship. Keeping the right balance when providing information and deciding what to disclose at which time requires some tact and skill on the side of the influencer marketing team or agency but it will help to ensure that you will not be filed away under 'boring'. Now isn't that something worth striving for?

Increase Investment in AR: What Would It Take

*A*nalyst Relations (AR) programs typically do not have sufficient resources (e.g., spokespeople bandwidth for analyst interactions, AR headcount, and budget) for the tasks at hand. Kea Company see underinvestment in AR pretty much across the board regardless of market (e.g., services, software, or hardware), geography, size, or stage of maturity.

This underinvestment by vendors that sell to large enterprises is puzzling because executives at those vendors frequently comment on the impact that the analysts have on sales deals. Kea Company strategists have personally been involved in many conversations with vendor executives where they did not just mention in passing the issue of analyst sales influence, but got very angry at a negative impact of the analysts. However, those same executives never made the connection between investing in AR and the return on investment (ROI) through top line revenue growth by mitigating negative commentary or leveraging positive commentary.

So what can AR teams do to get their companies to invest more in AR? Kea Company does not have a magic bullet for this, though we do have best practices and supporting tools. What we would like to do with this post is to solicit ideas from the AR professionals, other vendor staff, and analysts.

What do you think AR should be doing to convince their companies to invest more in influencing the analysts and supporting sales?

To get the ball rolling, here are a couple of Kea Company's high level suggestions:

▸ Ask your executive sponsor what it would require to obtain additional investment – It is interesting that many AR managers have never had a conversation with their executive sponsors asking a) what would AR have to do to warrant additional investment; and b) what are credible proof points that AR will have to develop. Once those items have been articulated AR would be in a better position to build a business case that specifically addresses the executive's requirements.

▸ Demonstrate economic impact by gathering data points on analyst influence on sales deals – For vendors that sell to large enterprises or large government organizations, advisory analysts typically have a significant influence at various points in the sales cycle. However, that influence does not surface for a variety of reasons, not the least of which is that nobody at the vendor is actively asking prospects about their sources of advice on major purchases and AR does not have a way gathering data from sales. In this case, AR should be harvesting sales impact data whether anecdotal in nature (e.g., getting deal information when a sales colleague calls asking for help) or systematically (e.g., surveying customer about their use of the analysts).

Bottom Line: Vendors are "leaving money on the table" by not investing appropriately in AR. It would be in both the AR community's and analysts' best interest to collaborate on ideas and best practices for how to develop a convincing business case for investment in AR.

"Best Practice" Ingredients in Analyst Relations

In any business environment the phrase 'best practice' sooner or later comes up when people are talking about planning, execution and measurement of business activities. According to Wikipedia "a best practice is a method or technique that has consistently shown results superior to those achieved with other means, and that is used as a benchmark. In addition, a "best" practice can evolve to become better as improvements are discovered."

So the concept is fairly straight forward but to establish what actually constitutes best practice in a specific context is anything but easy. In addition even knowing what the 'best practices' are doesn't necessarily meant that you know how to actually implement them in your specific environment. In today's blog post I want to look at 'best practices' in the context of analyst relations.

Getting started with analyst relations can prove to be quite a challenge if a company does not have any previous experience in dealing with analyst companies. The number of analysts who are covering a specific technology niche is usually limited so it is very hard to just get started and learn to do the job while you are doing it. Chances are that you will end up making some serious mistakes which – given the limited audience size – will prove to be very hard to correct. I have listened in, and helped prepare dozens of vendor presentations and analyst meetings. It is fair to say that the range of professionalism I have seen varies greatly. So working out the 'best practices' on your own will mean that you are taking quite a risk with the reputation of your company.

Now, what do we do when we don't know what to do? Right, you hire an expert who knows how things need to be done. Well, based on my experience this is not what will actually ensure that you are executing 'best practices'. Knowing what works and what doesn't and understanding the agenda of the various analyst firms and the individual analysts only helps to a certain degree. In my opinion 'best practice' in analyst relations is not based on finding that one magic bullet. Doing analyst relations this way is a static approach that amounts to pushing (un-customized) information in the direction of your target analysts without really building a relationship. It is my opinion that the 'best practices' for a vendor are a very individual thing that depends on the available resources (time, money and expertise) a company can "spare" for analyst relations, the technology niche the vendor is active in and the agility of the vendor (both in terms of innovation and in terms of growing the business). Only when balancing these factors will you be able to come up which an analyst relations program that will not only reach the analysts but will actually convince them. Having worked with many vendors throughout my time at an analyst firm and now as an analyst relations consultant I have seen some good and quite a few bad examples which have brought me to the conclusion that there is no way you can completely outsource your analyst relations program. Any truly successful analyst relations program will always be a highly customized joined effort which combines the know-how of the analyst landscape with the specific inside knowledge about your company. More than anything this means that 'best practices' in analyst relations are based on building the right team with both internal and external parties and staying flexible enough to adapt to changes in the market and analyst perception.

So if you are willing to compete in the field of analyst relations, make sure that you are well prepared and have all the resources in place to win the game. Trying to find the right way without staying engaged will not be enough when you are competing on a global level and when messing things up might mean that you won't get a second chance to fix things.

How To Eat
An Elephant –
A Recipe For Proper
Analyst Relations

*W*hen starting with analyst relations companies often realise that the task lying ahead of them is pretty daunting. There are several hundred analyst firms with thousands of analysts publishing research for every imaginable market niche. On the other side there are tens of thousands technology providers worldwide vying for the attention of these analysts. This means that simply having a great product will not be enough to get noticed.

But how does one cope with the task of sorting though this vast number and actually getting down to doing some work? This is where the proverbial elephant comes into play: **How does one eat an elephant? The answer is one bite at a time.** If the whole of the analyst community is too much to digest at once, it must be broken down into smaller pieces. So one of the main tasks of any analyst relations program will be to come up with a way to **structure and prioritise both the analyst firms and the analyst community** in a way that makes sense for your company and your analyst relations goals. Targeting analyst from the top three or four analyst companies that are experts in the technology your company is offering is the obvious thing to do. Doing this will give you a starting point but it also means that you will be omitting lots analysts that are just as important for the overall success of your analyst relations efforts. And since it is the obvious thing to do it will also mean that most of your competitors will be competing for the analysts' attention.

Having a clear cut idea what you want to achieve will also help you to build your list of analyst firms and analysts you will want to target. For example there are some analyst firms that have a great presence in the media but are lacking the client base to make them attractive as potential channels to directly impact the buying decisions of your buyers. So if you are looking to support your PR efforts and increase your presence in the media you might have to target a different set of analysts than if your main goal is to influence the analysts who are supporting your prospects in sorting through their vendor short list when making a buying decision. Pretty much the same applies for selecting analysts based on the verticals or geographical areas they are covering. All these criteria will help narrow down the number and allow you to come up with an initial list of analysts that are relevant for your analyst relations program.

However the problem with all these selection criterias is that you will not only need to come up with the right criteria to match your analyst relation goals, but they also require a deep understanding of the capabilities, methodologies and focus of the various analyst firms and analysts. Without this understanding chances are that you will waste a lot of effort dealing with the 'wrong' analysts wasting both time and money. So make sure that your cook knows how to properly prepare the elephant before it is served and eaten.

3 things Analyst Relations Managers need to know about Gartner in Africa

Sharon Robinson

Are you an Analyst Relations (AR) manager with a regional remit that includes Africa? Remain unconvinced of Gartner's influence at a regional level and unclear how to drive sales effectiveness? Here are three points to consider when designing your influencer programme.

1. **African enterprise Chief Information Officer (CIO) challenges are no different to their international peers'**

   It is true that Gartner does not have any analysts based in Africa, nor do they have a specific Africa coverage agenda such as those for India or China. This however, does not mean that Gartner has limited influence in the region.

   African CIO's face the same challenges as those of their peers abroad, and turn to Gartner for exactly the same reasons – a source of credible, independent expertise, steeped in IT best practice. Analyst, Mark Raskino, underscored this point following Gartner Africa's 2014 Symposium.

   The truth is African CIO's are crying out for skilled IT resources and often treat their investment in Gartner (and many of the large consulting firms) as a virtual extension of their existing teams, even if it does come with a hefty price tag. It is for this reason that Gartner Africa is now selling its services into approximately *12 African countries and is continually expanding its sales force on the ground in South Africa.

2. **The vertical industries investing**

   Gartner's regional spending split between end users and vendors is roughly 80/20. The most significant *proportion of the end user client base falls into the Banking and Investment vertical, which mirrors the most digitally savvy industry in the region, and not surprisingly, one's with the deepest pockets!

   Gartner's key African verticals (in order of priority) are:
   ▶ Banking and Investment
   ▶ Insurance
   ▶ Retail
   ▶ Energy and Utilities
   ▶ Manufacturing
   ▶ Media

The easiest way to determine topics and verticals of highest priority in region is by looking at the annual event calendar. Gartner's sales folks contribute directly to the prioritization of these events based on customer feedback.

AR managers should use their inquiry time to connect with the analyst presenters who regularly visit the region, as well as the vertical lead analysts, to arm their sales folks with contextualized content.

3. Understanding the Gartner CIO product portfolio

Whilst Gartner does not employ analysts in the region, they do employ a team of Executive Partner's (EP) to support their Executive Program (previously called the CIO Signature Program) client base, as well as a team of consultants. A common mistake is to confuse the role of the EP and consultants with that of the Gartner analysts.

The Executive Program solution is only available to Gartner end user clients. The sole purpose of the EP is to assist the CIO in achieving their key initiatives through access to Gartner's analyst and research resources and regular meetings.

A couple of points worth highlighting here are:

▶ The EP forms part of a global team of Gartner Executive Partners. The materials and tools that they use are those produced centrally by the Gartner IT Executive research team, most recently led by Dave Aron.

▶ The only individuals who can advise on vendor selection are analysts or consultants.

AR managers not already familiar with the product should build an understanding of the solution. Fundamentally, it is the materials and tools delivered through this product that the most senior IT end users are exposed to most.

Had any experience working with Gartner in other emerging markets? What role do you think that Analyst Relations has to play in the regional sales cycle?

* Gartner Africa is only permitted to service and sell to clients outside of South Africa in a remote capacity (i.e. no Gartner personnel, including analysts, are allowed to physically travel into any country except South Africa).
* Public Sector also makes up a significant percentage of Gartner Africa's client mix

IIAR's Tragic Quadrant Spotlights Overrated Analysts

*A*nalyst firms should pay serious attention to the Institute of Industry Analyst Relations' (IIAR) new Tragic Quadrant. The TQ spotlights some upstart firms that have successfully won much greater mindshare with many AR managers than their firms have in the market. Analyst firms can boost their position in future editions of the TQ through being easier to work with, through increasing their profile on social media, and by appearing more open to discussing with and learning from vendors.

About the TQ

On June 8th 2015, the IIAR published its first Tragic Quadrant. The TQ shows the perception, by around 60 vendors' analyst relations professionals, of the sales impact, relevance and ease of interaction with 14 analyst firms. The results confirm two worrying findings from the 1,100 respondents to the Analyst Value Survey. First, vendors mistakenly give some companies credit for much more impact on sales than buyers tell us they have. Second, other companies with much greater influence on the market are absent.

My Take

The Tragic Quadrant is a modest and, in the IIAR's words, "slightly cheeky" attempt to chart the most influential analyst firms. It fails to do that. As a comparison, the 2014 Analyst Value

Survey (AVS) collected the responses of 450 users of analyst research in demand-side organisations, those which buy IT. When we asked those end-users that firms influence buying, they mention both companies that get into the TQ's top 14 and many which do not. Everest and NelsonHall, for example, are highly rated by the demand-side in the AAS but are absent from the TQ. Also ignored are CXP Group, Aberdeen and ISG although end-users tell us those firms are influencing buyers notably. The IIAR's survey, however, places analyst firms like Constellation, ESG, SMB and Ventana in their top 14, when they fail to get into the top 20 in the AAS question.

The principal reason the TQ fails to show influence accurately is that AR people over-rate particular firms. While the survey design and execution could be improved, our warnings about IIAR surveys has been consistent over several years: don't forget who took the survey. AR people will always tend to equal being easy to influence with being impactful, and they will tend to overlook analyst firms that do not actively develop business with AR managers.

It succeeds, however, in showing those analyst firms that have high mindshare with the AR managers that took the survey. The value for vendors in this chart is the size of the bubbles, which shows how easy the firms are to interact with: use this as a guide to understand which firms are harder to crack.

The actual audience for the TQ should be the analyst firms. Everest and NelsonHall have every right to snigger over the inclusion of SMB and ESG, but they should be asking instead why they don't have a higher profile in the AR community, especially in North America.

The context

While the TQ is new, the ideas have been brewing for a while. The data some from a survey conducted irregularly over the last several years by the IIAR. The primary output is the Analyst of the Year award. The term Tragic Quadrant has been coined previously to refer to the Magic Quadrant ironically.

The article announcing the TQ credits Helen Chantry. Back in 2013, Chantry and I discussed the Analyst Value Survey and the KCG Mystical Box, which the TQ seems also to pay homage to. Helen wasn't able to answer some questions I emailed her about the survey last year, but I've picked a few things up. The base of respondents is rather small: many IIAR members were invited to take part, but not all, and the survey was open for only a day or two. Some of the criteria are hard to grasp. The TQ segments firms into being 'global' and being 'independent': only one firm is described as both although, as far as I can see, these words seem to have no identifiable meaning.

For the IIAR team that produced the survey, a key factor was the ease of interacting with analyst firms. They wrote that *"analyst firms should monitor the 'transactional tax' they impose on AR people: if they raise the 'interaction barrier' too high while not providing sufficient coverage and not showing impact, their vendor information source might soon provide them only a partial view of the market (raising exhaustivity and fairness issues) or their vendor revenues might suffer too."*

Analyst firms need to pay attention to that notion, even if they don't accept it. Partly this is a side-swipe at firms like Gartner whose requests for ever-increasing volumes of information don't lead to any improvement in research quality or favourability. But it is in some way a representation of what is creating the unusual vision of the market shown in the TQ. How is is possible to leave off Everest and ISG and yet include Ventura and SMB? The answer must surely be in the ease of interaction. Probably those two firms are reaching more frequently to AR people and are adding value to the relationships they are building with AR people.

The bottom line

▸ The TQ repeats a finding of the AVS: the vendor community greatly misunderstands which firms are impacting on sales.

▸ AR professionals should not use this diagram to guide them on the impact or relevance of these firms. It is misleading, incomplete and inaccurate.

▸ AR professionals should pay attention to the estimates that this chart makes of the relative ease of interacting with firms. Pad your plan for time to get through to these companies, and recover from them. Most importantly, please appreciate that a firm that is hard to work with is often much more influential and has demanding communications because of robust methods.

▸ If ESG can get into the IIAR's top ten, then any firm with a couple of dozen analysts on Twitter can. Analyst firms should consider if they want to be a top performer on this chart's future editions.

▸ Analyst Firms should understand that this shows the opinions of 60 or so AR pros. If they are an important group of stakeholders, you need to be adding more value to AR people and lubricating the interactions with them.

Making Music Together: The 4 C's of an Analyst Inquiry

Christopher Manfredi

> *You can discover more about a person in an hour of play than in an hour of conversation*
> *– Plato*

In 1957, a confident (and maybe cocky) young lead singer of a new rock band met another young musician, a guitarist around his same age, introduced by a mutual friend. They immediately hit it off, sharing their love of American rock and roll and singing songs. The young guitarist showed the singer how to tune his guitar and displayed his virtuoso guitar playing. The guitarist was almost too good thought the singer; he might still his spotlight. He relented, however, and brought the new guitarist into his band. It was for good that the cocky front man brought him on though. It made for a happier world.

John Lennon and Paul McCartney had come together.

There's a lot you can get out of chance meetings and stories shared; good conversations spur good ideas. In the book *The Power of Pull: How Small Moves Smartly Made Can Set Big Things in Motion*, authors John Hagel III, John

Seely Brown and Land Davison write that the companies that are going to shape the future will develop it through creative collaboration. Creation spaces and engaging conversations lead to big ideas. **Talking to someone about something interesting is the catalyst sometimes for big things.**

An inquiry with an intelligent business or technology analyst can be one such catalyst, and it's a definitely a two-way street. Analysts, and the firms they work for, spend tireless hours researching and developing their knowledge, but they cannot get a complete picture unless they speak to those in the business, visiting the "factory floors". Vendors may spend all their waking hours toiling at making the world a more productive and efficient place through technology, but unless they know how their technology compares in the marketplace or even what the marketplace wants, their hours toiling may be spent in vain.

Working your way into engaging conversations may be easy for some scruffy young musicians with little care but Little Richard songs, but for others, it may prove more difficult. It's a busy time in the world. Between the research deadlines, events, and writing of analysts and the sales calls, management meetings, and jet lag of vendors, it's tough answering emails and jumping on the phone.

Inquiries, though, still must be pursued to find an audience for a company's ideas and market initiatives. In today's high-paced tech world, an analyst's kudos could make or break deals for many a service provider, so knowing how to make the most out of an inquiry is key to building a company's internal knowledge and outside thought leadership.

How does one find a chance to make "music" between two busy strangers? Prepare and plan by following the 4 C's of Inquiries: **Comfort, Converse, Connect, and Continue**.

Comfort:

One of the tenets of Dale Carnegie was always to be friendly. His seminal book, *How To Win Friends And Influence People,* said that some of the best ways to make people comfortable to you was to give **sincere appreciation, smile, be a good listener and always use the person's name**.

While it may be difficult to smile through a telephone inquiry, vendors can make an effort to make the analyst comfortable by getting to know them before the call and show graciousness for even participating. After short introductions from the members on the conversations, speaking on the analyst's recent research or blog post is a good way to showing the analyst that you are prepared.

The first few moments in the conversation can make or break the comfort level so be sure to be ready. Some things to remember before you enter a call:

▸ Have an analyst profile: Know who they are, what they cover, and what they're interested in. Mention some highlights possibly of their career or alma mater.
▸ Read over their work: Sharing a view on recent research lets the analyst know that not only are you interested

in learning but you already have been learning.
▸ Give setting for call: Giving a short synopsis of why you are speaking sets the analyst up for what is going to be talked about and sets him or her at ease.

Converse:

In the book *The Art of Conversation*, the seemingly effortless human activity of talking has been broken down to five distinct points:
1. **Put others at ease**
2. **Put yourself at ease**
3. **Weave in all parties**
4. **Establish shared interests**
5. **Actively pursue your own**

While our Comfort stage may have already taken care of those first two, the last three should definitely be a part of an inquiry.

Having multiple parties is good on a call, but make sure to have 2-3 people interacting at the max. It's off putting to try and bring that many people and their questions into the conversation. Additionally, too many people means less of a chance for the analyst to talk which is what you exactly want.

Remember that the most important information in an inquiry is new information. The less you speak and the more you listen, the better chance you have of learning something notable. Let the analyst speak and you will find an even more engaging and excited analyst. Analysts spend all day researching and understanding about something very specific. **They are excited to have their voices heard. Let them stay excited.**

As they speak and get engaged, be sure to pepper questions that lead to multiple layers. Make sure to go for the interesting ones and make sure Yes/No questions should be taken removed from your list.

You did create a list of questions to keep the conversation going, right?

Connect:

Research has found that with a serious topic or a good friend, we measure a conversation's success by how enthralled we were by what the other person said is another thought seen in *The Art of Conversation*.

Being enthralled by someone, however, is no easy feat.

The real secret in it is that you are the one in charge of ensuring they are enthralling you. The way to really "connect" is by making sure you drive the conversation to where it needs to go. **Remember, you called the meeting; you are in charge of the flow.**

I have been in inquiries and seen individuals lose their patience with an analyst when things aren't going right or when an analyst might not be giving them the exact information they require.

This is why Connect is the hardest of these stages; it takes a deft facilitator to find the connecting point between people. This could be their love of a technology, their business savvy, their knowledge of marketplace or their favorite sports team. **It doesn't matter because it's up to the inquirer to get the most out of the inquiry.**

Establishing and keeping a healthy rapport throughout is tantamount. Dead air or no talking during an inquiry can kill the flow of conversation. Being abrupt or rude can never happen.

To truly connect, you have to find the catalyst point for combined interest which you should have already found out through the profile of the analyst. Understand what they know and what you think they want to share. Ask them the right questions and lead them to the information you know they have. That's how you (and they) will really connect.

Continue:

The easiest stage in the inquiry process is often the most missed. **Ending the inquiry is not ending the relationship; an inquiry is just the start.**

You have to leave the conversation with the next action to complete the inquiry process.

An analyst's work is never done. It doesn't matter how many research reports, tweets, or blog posts they write because that's what they get paid to do: write. What that ultimately means is that they continually are looking for ammo for their cannons.

For a vendor, the best time to ask what they're needing or looking to write up next is when they are right in front of you. The most important thing to an analyst is information, new information. So feel free to ask them what else they may want to do or what they might need such as:

▸ A briefing from company in their domain
▸ A collaborative project
▸ A visit to your office for a more intimate chat

Just ending a conversation abruptly with no follow up takes the "relations" out of analyst relations. Make sure you keep the relationship going.

Active and fun conversations can be organic but orchestrated; it can really happen. It's up to those in it to make it desirable for both parties.

Inquiries are just one of the keys to understanding more about a subject, the business environment, or even your own company's standing and your interaction could be more important than you think. You are a reflection of your company in that moment, so you must seize it. Prepare for your inquiry well, pace yourself throughout, and make sure to stay engaged.

Most of all though, have fun. You never know what kind of music you will create.

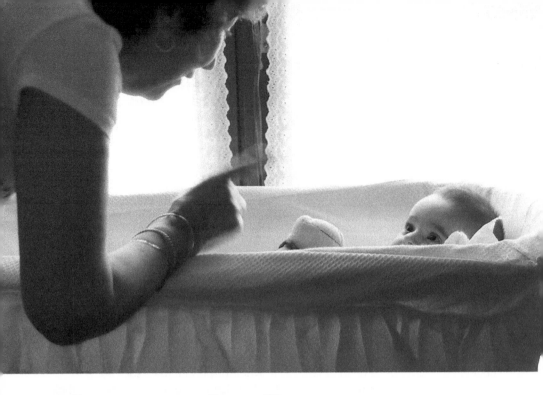

The Tao of Influence: Part One

Allyson Casey

WHY INFLUENCERS MATTER Want to know the quickest way to kill a conversation? Begin and end with your undisputed awesomeness. Too harsh? Perhaps, but sometimes the truth hurts.

Winning the hearts and minds of customers is an opportunity for a conversation. The catch is, the conversation isn't always between you and the customer. Other people and groups influence customer decisions, often more heavily than we'd like to admit.

Have you ever made a major purchase decision based solely on what you saw in an ad or on the company's website? No other convincing necessary, the ad copy and value proposition were enough. I'd wager you can count the number of times you have done this on one hand.

Most people check information sources they *trust* before a purchase decision. According to global PR agency Edelman, the three most trusted resources the average person has are: **Friends, Family and "Experts."**

Every year as part of the Trust Barometer survey, Edelman takes the collective population's temperature on how much they trust, or distrust different information sources.

The 2015 survey turned in some results that I think are particularly relevant.

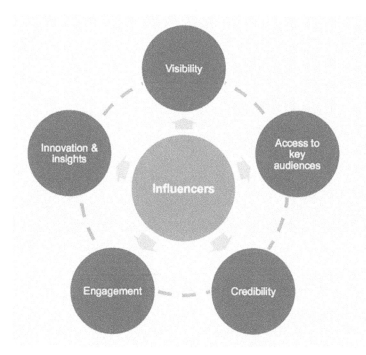

- **68 percent of those surveyed recommended** a company that they trusted to a friend or colleague.
- **80 percent bought** a product or service because they trusted the company behind it.

Now, friends and family lead this list of most trusted. But what about those "experts," those "other influencers?"

Trusted Influencers as I call them, offer a unique opportunity to generate word of mouth and help build trust in your company and products. Notice, I'm talking about what they offer, as opposed to who they are.

In reality you could put a wide variety of groups or people at the center, customers, developers, partners, industry analysts or associations all fit the bill. The group or groups to focus on will depend on your business needs.

Trusted Influencers Offer:

- **Visibility:** Remember the marketing rule of 7? A prospect needs to see or hear about your brand seven times before things click.
- **Access to Audiences** you care about. Think of this as another door into the conversation with your potential customers.
- **Credibility:** It's one thing to say you're product is awesome- it's another for someone else to say it.
- **Engagement** outside the purchase "funnel" – for example trainings.
- **Innovation & Insight**: a feedback loop, which in my experience can often be more candid than simply asking customers directly.

Great, we know what they offer. Now, how do you get them to work with you? Hint, there will be horses, references to 80's hair care products and a framework for engaging influencer audiences. Tune in for part two soon!

The Tao of Influence: Part Two

Allyson Casey

A FRAMEWORK FOR WINNING THE HEARTS AND MINDS OF TRUSTED IN-FLUENCERS.

In my last post I outlined why influencing the influencers matters. In short, trusted influencers- specifically those beyond media- are a powerful lever in reaching customers and building trust in your brand. Ok, so how does one successfully build a relationship with such influential groups?

Think like the Horse Whisperer

If you've ever ridden a horse you know, you can't just tell a horse to do something. That's upward of a half ton of pure power and will! It has to trust you, there has to be a partnership between horse and rider. The only way to build that kind of trust is through **deliberate and consistent interaction**, it's a long game. But, once that partnership is forged, it's a beautiful thing.

The same is true of building a re-lationship with an influencer group. It's not about pushing product first, it's about taking the time to build a partnership. Here's the framework I developed for working with influencers of all stripes.

Step One: Listen

If I learned anything in 10 years at Intuit, it was to focus on the customer. In this case it's your "trusted Influencer."

▸ Where are they and who else is talking to them?

▸ What are they actually asking you for?

▸ Is what they need something you (or someone you know) can provide?

▸ What can you offer in terms of help or connections? (Hint: Not just product.)

Remember, how you go about listening and engaging matters. Influence and trust are not transactional. **Interactions need to be genuine.** Nobody likes a used car salesman! *If you're interested in some good additional reading, Geoffrey Colon posted a great* *update on authenticity in marketing that is well worth a read.*

Step Two: Partner

Show up s as a partner, a true advocate, and make the influencer you're working with the hero. Simply put, enable them to better serve the customers you have in common. Remember those old Vidal Sassoon ads from the 80's?

Step Three: Measure & Market

Thought leadership is lovely, but it has to be in service to generating an activity or outcome to truly matter. That said, the ability to measure outcomes and movement are critical. How else will you be able to mark progress? A bit of hard learned wisdom, don't expect your influencer partner to want or to be able to capture the data that's important to you. Minimizing the burden on your influencer partner should be top of mind.

Do yourself a favor build a clear path to "action" and a mechanism for measurement into your influencer activities at the outset. Read: don't just hand your influencers valuable content and hope they use it for social media. Plant the seed of the idea and suggest they use the content for a social campaign, even include some sample Tweets: *"We'd love for you to use this on your social channels…"* This also gives you a chance to pay it forward and elevate what your influencers are sharing.

Which brings me to Market. This is the first real test of the partnership with the influencer. If all is going well, you've established a two way street where it is both easy to talk about the benefits of working with you and at the same time, an opportunity for you to elevate the work your influencer partner is doing.

Remember, a rising tide carries all ships!

Gartner and Forrester are not, repeat not, Tier 1

*Y*ou read the headline correctly; Forrester and Gartner should never be considered Tier 1. Yes, yes, Gartner is the industry behemoth, and Forrester is likely the number two firm for enterprise end users, but that does not make them automatically Tier 1 for the purpose of creating a ranked and tiered analyst list.

In the analyst list methodology our firm has developed, analyst firms should not be given an automatic "tier" because what should be ranked is analysts, not firms. Ranking should be done based on a set of criteria (e.g., industry visibility, research coverage, client base, and so on) related to the vendor's and AR team's objectives. After a ranked list is created, then AR draws lines on the list to split the list into groups (e.g., Tier 1, 2 and 3, or strategic, important, and secondary or whatever you want to call them). That will define the types the service level (e.g., 1-to-1, 1-to-many or none-to-many responses) the AR team will give each analyst on the list. Tiers and service levels are created based on AR resources (i.e., the bigger the AR team, the more Tier 1 analysts can be supported). While the characteristics of the firm will contribute to the data for ranking, merely working at Forrester or Gartner should never guarantee an analyst that they will have Tier 1 status.

Our strategists frequently see analyst relations (AR) teams give Tier 1 status to analysts of the Big Two, even if their true relevance should place them much farther down on the ranked list. This can lead to AR misallocating resources by putting too much emphasis on some analysts while not having sufficient resources to brief or respond to other analysts. Remember, depending on the market and the analysts, a single practitioner or boutique can have just as much influence as the Big Two.

Our Technique:

▶ Develop (or use our) analyst list management methodology that uses a mix of weighted criteria

▶ Work with your internal stakeholders to set the criteria and weights as well as obtain buy-in for the final ranked list

▶ Set service levels based on AR resources

▶ Be disciplined – but diplomatic – about adhering to service levels even when lower ranked analysts directly contact you

Bottom Line: Few if any AR teams have the unlimited resources required to support every request from every analyst. AR needs to develop a methodology for ranking analysts based on relevance to the company's objectives. Then AR needs to split the ranked list into groups with the sizes of the groups based on the resources AR has available. Finally, AR needs to ensure that its internal stakeholders are in agreement with the ranking methodology and service level framework so that AR will not have problems adhering to the service levels when an analyst calls an executive to complain about their treatment.

Analyst Relations is Not a Billion Dollar Club

If we would receive a free lunch every time a Tech SME owner says "So you are in Analyst Relations, so mainly high-end customers, right?", we'd be eating for free the rest of our lives. Why is this perception there? Why don't people see that Analyst Relations is not about how many employees a company has or how high the revenue is. You don't have to own a big office and be on top of the world (yet). In every stage there is value to be added by communicating with analysts worldwide.

It is all about what you have to offer, and how you can communicate that to the world. It isn't about what your competition is doing or how big they are in comparison to you. Of course it all relates to one another, but these should not be the reason not to undertake the steps needed to communicate to the outside world via the professional channels. You need to benchmark your vision and product with outsiders who's job it is to know what is happening in the world. These analysts judge you based on their twenty something years of experience. Yes they can be critical, but that is what you look for in feedback. If you can't handle that, quit being an entrepreneur.

If you feel that you don't need any help than that is completely up to you. Personally I don't think it is about needing help, but leveraging every opportunity you get and about making an extra effort to introduce your company to the world via independent experienced professionals, who know what they are talking about. Yes they are still only human, but we all have our core business and this is how we help each other. Make a 25K reservation in your budget and show the world what you have to offer, you'll end up saving time and money. Working smart, efficient and listening to others is something anyone can do, not just billion dollar companies.

How Valuable is Service?

*H*ow do you measure whether clients are happy with your service? Do we need a matrix to make sure we make it all visible, or can we just conclude that when you ask the question their response has to speak for itself?

Every company claims that they deliver the best service or say that they are all about service. But considering our growth in new clients in the past years, that doesn't seems to be the only thing clients look for. So how good is your service and how much time should you spend on it? All valid questions, but that doesn't make it easier.

One thing we can all agree on, is that it differs per country. Certain countries in Asia don't care too much about service, so selling on service in their domestic region is a waste of sales efforts. In North America service is important. In Europe it really depends on where you are and what your selling.

So if you have a base product that needs simple execution worldwide, maybe it is all in the sales pitch. Some clients care and some don't. Apart from the location where you are selling, it also depends on your product or service. In our business it is all about communication, openness and working flexible hours. Most of all, just get it done. Fix it! It makes life simple in my opinion. So why are there still so many competitors that talk about service instead of price, when the only outcome is that clients expect you to "fix it".

I love service myself. I think it is common sense to add it in your contract and talk about it. But maybe, just maybe, it is not the number one factor for clients to choose you.

Engage

How to communicate with analysts

How industry analysts can come to briefings better prepared

In private conversations, Influencer Relations professionals often critique the analysts' level of preparedness for a briefing. However, the IR pros are unwilling to actually say something to the analyst for fear of hurting the relationship or courting retaliation. We think that these fears are unfounded as most analysts would appreciate reasonable suggestions for how they can improve what they do.

To get the ball rolling here are few ideas that should only take an analyst a few minutes to do immediately prior to a briefing:

▶ Review the information or materials that the vendor has (hopefully) sent you regarding the briefing.
▶ Review notes on past briefings from this vendor
▶ Use Google News to quickly scan recent headlines for potential surprises
▶ Visit the vendor's webpage and quickly scan recent press releases
▶ If the vendor is a public company, quickly review the relevant parts of the most recent financial announcement
▶ Jot down recent relevant end-user comments about the vendor to get you in the frame of mind to ask targeted questions
▶ If this is a product or services briefing review similar offerings from competitive vendors

Now some analysts might react to these suggestions thinking it adds a lot of work to a briefing which they are not "paid to do". It is Kea Company's opinion that this should not be a lot of work – and that the information you are receiving from the vendor helps in your overall client research and therefore has a lot of value. If you have an ongoing relationship with this vendor this should be a very easy process. If this is an unfamiliar vendor you might ask for some of the information when accepting the briefing. In either case, take the time to review all materials from the vendor before the briefing starts.

Bottom line: Analysts should prepare themselves appropriately when accepting a vendor briefing. Hopefully the information received will add to the overall understanding of the market strategy, products, and services that are available to the clients of the analyst firm.

Question: Are you getting the most from your analyst contracts? Kea Company can help. Our strategists can:

▶ Evaluate the usage of your contracted analyst services and suggest ways to maximise business value from your investment
▶ Train your colleagues with analysts seats (e.g., Gartner Advisory and Forrester Roleview) through efficient and effective distance learning via webinar or teleconference
▶ Critique your upcoming analyst contracts to ensure you are getting the right services from the right firms to meet your business needs
▶ Save you time, money and aggravation

You do not need to spend hours on the phone or ask you procurement department for thousands of dollars to start the conversation with Kea for those immediate results. Contact us to learn more!

This post originally appeared on LinkedIn. Here are some of the points from the discussion that followed the publication:

Mohy Shams from Gartner shared: Thanks for sharing your comments. I think it's great advice, however in reality I'm not sure if this would happen. From my personal experience working at Gartner (SMB vendors & Larger accounts), I feel analysts have too much on their agenda to take out more time to conduct this type of preperation for a vendor briefing. Baring in mind, an analyst is not required to take a VB unless it will be of value to the end user clients they advise or if they havent heard of the vendors name before & been mentioned several times by multiple end user clients (or if the vendor sounds cool, genuinely interesting for the analyst and isn't another 'Me Too' vendor!). Therefore, the vendor really needs to differentiate themselves amongst others wanting to raise mindshare of anaysts. I think it would be great if you could share your thoughts on how vendors could create thought leadership / mindshare with analysts using unconventional methods. Once again, these are just my personal opinions, not of Gartners officially.

Samyr Jriri of Kea Company replied: On one hand, vendors indeed should make sure their vendor briefing is relevant through good prep and strong alignment to the coverage areas. What vendors often forget is that a vendor briefing – in the first place – is about adding value to the end users through the analyst ecosystem, and not about themselves. Mostly when challenges around the vendor briefing process are identified and discussed, the focus tends to go to what the vendor has done wrong, often with good reason. However this post is about what the analysts can/should do from their side, what is good vendor preparation for if it isn't consumed prior to a briefing? Your point about analysts often not having time is valid in so far that it is a reality, however it is not valid as an excuse. Where vendors need to keep improving the quality of their interactions with analysts, analysts need to make sure their quality doesn't get compromised because of high volume pressure from above (which is where the time restraints mostly come from). Unfortunately, these are the consequences when pushing too much on hardcore data driven business growth in what essentially is a relationship driven people business.

Christian Holscher from BT: Agree with you Thom. And adding to Samyrs point (ultimately it's not about the vendor, it's about the value for the end customer) I found briefings to be most valuable when the analysts freed themselves from just ranking a vendor against "market standards" or the benchmark set by some market share leader. Instead the best analysts explored how this specific vendor interpreted the market in their own way and in the light of what they understand of the challenges and ambitions of their target audience. In the end this approach may touch the same criteria – but it's a very different mindset and helps to discover value outside the box. Some analysts aim to rank vendors against a standardised set of criteria, often defined by the market leaders – and this has some value if you're in a commodity market. But if you try to find a vendor that fits your specific context and your strategy, then you want an analyst who appreciates diversity. The vendor preparation you suggest communicates professional respect and makes a briefing more effective. An analysts curiosity for how vendors see the market and their ability to differentiate how vendors apply capabilities differently to market challenges and to customer ambitions makes their insight truly valuable. By the way also for the vendor in terms of being challenged to best explain their proposition.

Measured in Minutes:
The ROI of an Analyst Briefing

As part of the ongoing struggle to convince their management about the value of analyst relations, AR professionals often prove the effectiveness of their AR programmes by showing written research with mentions about the vendor. This type of metric is often shortsighted because it does not take into account the verbal delivery of research via informal conversations over the phone and at analyst conferences.

Because the IT industry analysts that focus on advising IT managers (e.g., 451, Forrester and Gartner) are on the phone every day with their clients, the ROI for a briefing can be nearly instantaneous. It is common for an analyst to finish an IT vendor briefing and use the information in the very next call. In fact, the analyst will do a little name dropping with the end-user client to show how wired-in they are (e.g., "… funny you should mention CSI tools I just got off the phone with its VP of Services where I learned how it is taking care of its professional services quality. I believe you can now add CSI to your short list with minor risk. …").

Analyst relations professionals need to educate their executives on how the analysts deliver their research and advice (i.e., one-on-one inquiry, formal presentations and written research). By doing so, AR can start to move executives away from focusing on the written research as the only method for measuring AR effectiveness.

Our process: The next time you schedule analyst briefings, call the analysts in advance and ask them to help educate the executive that will be doing the briefing. Then, during the briefing ask the analysts about how they use the information from a briefing. Drill down by asking whether they think that they'll be using the information gathered on inquiries with end users. This should then open up the conversation for a few minutes about how end users leverage analyst recommendations and analysis.

Bottom Line: Often IT vendor executives question the value of briefing the analysts when it seems like the analysts take months – if at all – to write about the information provided in the briefing. Regardless if the analysts ever write about a vendor, the information provided could be used within minutes of your briefing during a phone inquiry with a corporate IT buyer – your customer.

Seven Mistakes That Kill Pitches To Analysts

*A*s part of our Influencer Pitch Process research, 44 people at analyst pitches (on either side of the table) told us about times when the meetings went badly wrong. Seven mistakes came up time and time again. Indeed, everyone who commented mentioned at least one of these seven errors.

1. **Pitching in solutions that don't relate to the analyst's or customers' interests.**
2. **Using sales presentations or investor decks that give numbers and corporate fluff, but no emotion or customer proof.**
3. **Bad timing, especially talking for too long about background to really deliver a coherent narrative or roadmap.**
4. **Over-talking the potential upside for a solution or a market niche, both in terms of the pace and the scale of adoption.**
5. **Trying to force a technology into a market segment where it does not best fit.**
6. **Not seeming to be open to questions or negative feedback.**
7. **Looking down on, or paying too little attention to, women analysts.**

Anticipate Relevant Outcomes Through New Media – It isn't difficult

Suyog Shetty

*e*ngaging with analysts brings in a variety of expectations. The most common and easily anticipated outcome is a positive report on the service provider; ironically not a balanced report. Any negative will be viewed as a potent explosive, and every effort will be undertaken to dilute or soften the 'blow'. The truth however remains, unchanged!

With the pervasive forces in the ecosystem indicating how the Airbnb's and Uber's are now changing the dynamics of the game, every other exec would like to draw an analogy to these enterprising, gutsy organizations. The fundamentals of their success remains applicable here as well – Engage with stakeholders and set the right expectations in countries of operations.

A lot of these are easier said than done. All the theories that apply for firms to be successful in this and the next era – the mantra of Collaborate,

Cooperate, Cohesiveness have already been successfully used with analysts by several service providers. These remain the critical must-haves of success when building meaningful relationships with analysts.

Leverage effectively – the platforms are right in front of you

Several opportunities today exist when AR professionals wish to leverage relationships with analysts that cover multiple businesses. The basic 'R's will continue to remain invaluable – *Reports, Recommendations, References*; but new mediums bring forth enormous opportunity; such as leveraging Twitter elaborating how useful you found responses to the Enquiry.

Or write a brief post on LinkedIn, appreciating the refreshing insights received during the analyst breakfast session – which was handy for your SBU head. Or retweet the purchased report, with relevant bite-sized comments that would be useful for everyone in the industry. Several of my recent learnings have been through retweets that brought essentials data points to my table instantly. Don't let twitter handles be the prerogative of the Corporate 'social media team', don't let these remain dormant with pithy facts – but get them activated to make it much more interesting, nugget-driven and refreshed.

Not just for external folks, but aim and repeat for internal stakeholders as well. Your internal communications team would be more than happy to partner with you and provide the necessary support for mailers, creatives that can be extremely powerful for several leaders. Every firm would have platforms such as yammer, news bulletins, messenger boards and so on. Don't forget, it will also be a huge educative process and get rousing support for all the efforts and acknowledgment received by analysts. This results into a huge cascading effect – which in turn brings out even newer, unheard of customer success stories, innovation undertaken by a bunch of reticent geeks in a store room, a novel approach for a faster go-to-market, a new solution that needs validation which you could take to the analysts, and so much more.

You pay analyst firms for these anyway, why not use the services. Analysts will love every such single opportunity that you take to them. They thrive on such instances, and thereby you'll build a stronger bond and quicker recall.

AR teams have to doggedly, and consistently take multiple steps to ensure they reach audiences with a simple and a non-overwhelming approach. What needs to be done is to move up from the stereotype platforms and go on a war footing leveraging new mediums. You will have critics who will not support or haggle, but once you strengthen your lasers with adequate substance, the organization's engines will rev up to support all your initiatives and be willing to go out of the way to support your efforts.

Wouldn't it be a stronger reinforcement yet again, which reflects how AR takes every trending element available and get the maximum return on time investment – when implemented simply and effectively?

Five Ways To Get a Better Deal From Gartner

Most vendors that subscribe to Gartner are being offered expanded services. Their proposed fees are also expanding. We have observed some common tactics and experiences within its client base. However, the central pressures are not in dealing with Gartner: the severe difficulty for AR directors and other Gartner clients is now to communicate internally.

Gartner's stock price tripled over five years, from around $40 in 2012 to around $120 in June 2017.

Its shares have never been higher. This rise partly reflects both share repurchases and growing profitability. Some of our clients think that the additional improvement may be largely due to increased profitability on a smaller number of customers.

If our clients are to believed, Gartner gets the lion's share of the added value created by increasing the average value of vendor renewals. Many vendors feel they are paying more for services they don't need, or never had to pay a premium for previously. They need to move beyond intractability.

Much of the frustration is with Gartner's role-based views of research. Forrester's role-based services introduced a substantially new research agenda supporting new questions of deep interest to specific roles. Some clients feel that Gartner's services are simply views on already-existing research that highlight research thought to be of interest to people in that position. The services seem to provide similar research, but more highly priced.

The self-confidence of vendors in pushing back at these sharp prices rises differs widely. Vendors spending less than $500,000 seem to be more anxious at disappointing Gartner; they mistakenly worry that their firm's standing in Gartner research would fall if they reduce their spending with the leading analyst firm. Vendors spending more than $500,000 have more self-confidence. They are more likely to feel that Gartner analysts' interest in their organisation won't change just because their spending on Gartner doesn't match that firm's expectations.

Much of the vendors' worries seems to rest on the wholly mistaken idea that Gartner is price-gouging. Instead, Gartner is trying to find ways to increase the value it offers to vendors. Of course, it also aims to ensure that providers' fees reflect the actual cost of serving them by closing down loopholes.

That said, revenue and profitability will remain key management metrics across the Gartner organisation. Executives are looking for increased profit: and means revenue has to increase faster than costs. They want to see that outcome from their sales managers — and without surprises. Account managers certainly face strong expectations to drive up the value of deals with vendors. They also want no surprises, so they must aim to communicate Gartner's expectations clearly. Account handlers also need to be brave enough to reset managers' expectations when clients seem unlikely to match the suggested increase.

All of that means that communication is crucial to the negotiation process. Sadly, the negotiating and influencing skills of research buyers are often limited. They often spring unhappy surprises on Gartner:

and the surprise is more likely to damage rapport than the actual decision. Some of the generic rules of negotiating are highly valuable in these discussions:

The first one to name a price gains the advantage.

Negotiators need to focus on interests, not positions.

Both sides need to understand their best alternative to a negotiated agreement in advance.

If the future value of the deal is disputed, propose contingent fees where the final value rises or falls in line with the value the solution is finally found to provide.

If it's late for everyone to be happy this year, start now to set expectations about next year.

Participants need to look beyond reason, and anticipate emotional concerns in the negotiation.

As I mentioned at the start, the real issue for AR managers is communicating internally. This has five aspects.

Counter 'pay to play'. The sharp increases in expenditure mean that managers negotiating with Gartner may have to negotiate internally with powerful stakeholders. Some managers will assume that Gartner's fee is a like a license to operate, and that a change in expenditure should lead to an equal change in the volume of positive mentions of their firm by Gartner. This assumption is a mistaken view that is especially common in organisations that have used cash to stimulate Gartner's attention, for example by buying advisory days, in the place of building a real rapport with Gartner analysts.

Focus on value, not cost. Colleagues have to understand that the question is: what is the value of the additional services in the Gartner portfolio? They need to be assured that the decision produces no analyst bias: otherwise they will focus on the cost, and not the value.

Measure comparative value. Opportunities have to found to assess the relative value of Gartner: usage statistics from Gartner.com and inquires are useful. However, surveys of internal users of Gartner services can produce compelling information about the satisfaction and insight that Gartner provides. These are powerful data for communicating with both Gartner and with colleagues.

Identify options. Internal and external providers of complementary and substitute services need to be assessed. Some managers will think that $500,000 can be turned into a 20- or 30-strong team of Indian or Filipino researchers who could provide equal value to Gartner. What alternatives are viable? How far does the firm have internal intelligence groups, sources of trusted second opinions and confidence in reducing the level of services from Gartner?

Neither take it nor leave it. Finally, is it just an all or nothing choice? Some vendors feel as if they either pay the increased rate or just put their subscription on hold so they can save up enough to subscribe at the higher rate later on. Some firms have suspended their subscriptions by paying ad hoc for Gartner reports and advisory sessions with analysts. Others accept much of the price increase but then try to increase the value of the deal even further, until they feel the added fee is justified.

Four Psychological Strategies for Analyst Relations

hristian Hampel, a researcher from the Psychologische Institut Mainz, and I have a totally new analyst relations strategy. Since February, we have been developing and testing some ideas from social psychology in conversations with industry analysts, AR people and a range of academic researchers.

Each of our four strategies is designed for companies in different stages of growth and market orientation. There is a strong parallel between these four stages and the four quadrants of the Influencer Quadrant, which we first published in 2012.

▶ **Spring.** When firms first meet the analysts, they are rising fast but from a low base. By virtue of their growing market presence not only is their share of voice growing, but also the firm's AR managers and spokespeople carry with them an assertive quality. They might be offering some new solutions, and often quite different expertise, but their clumsy and inconsistent tactics make them hard to trust.

▶ **Summer.** As growing firms approach their peak, they remain assertive but switch their approach. Earlier firms can take a mercenary approach, hoping to get insight and leads from analysts with little in exchange. In their peak, they develop more of a partnership approach towards industry analysts.

They remain assertive but start to work in a win-win way.

- **Autumn.** This is where strategy makes the biggest difference, and it's generally where the best analyst relations teams develop. These are organisations that are at their peak, or are growing mainly through M&A. Their dynamic is shifting between market growth and market defence. As a result, they need to be building very strong relationships with analysts and emphasising clients' switching costs.

- **Winter.** This is the crucial end-game for firms, when they come into high-stakes M&A as a way of life. In this period, firms are strongly on the defensive, but the passage into winter is often signaled by the move from a win-win approach to AR into much more confrontation, hard-ball transactional approaches. Often this is when the firm moves from one set of key analysts to another.

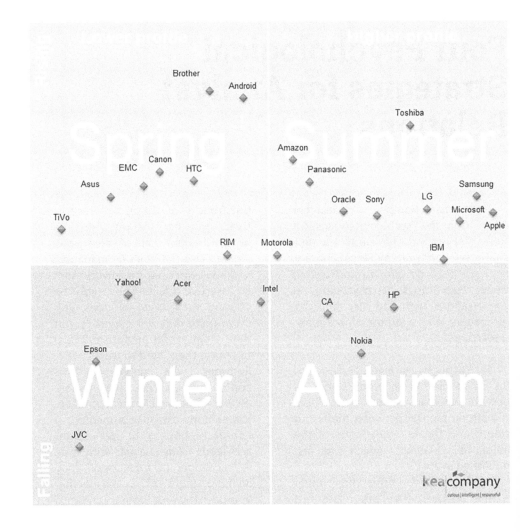

Insider Tips For Making The Most of Analyst Briefings

Rebecca Lieb

*A*s a research analyst covering digital technology, companies routinely (to the tune of up to a dozen per day) reach out to request briefings — even if that's not the terminology they use. It might be an "informational meeting," "our CEO would like to meet you," or "an advance look at the new product-or-feature we're launching."

You can call them what you want to. In the analyst community, they're briefings. The best ones provide value on both sides: to both the analysts and researchers, as well as to the tech firm (or in my case, agency or publisher, too, as I cover advertising and media).

We analysts conduct briefings to further our research agendas. We constantly monitor developments and companies that operate in our sphere of coverage. We're looking for trends and patterns, for case studies, and often, to make introductions or connections between businesses or people operating in the same sphere who really ought to know one another. (This has more than once led to investments, acquisitions and partnerships.) Analysts are influencers and a form of media; we might write about your clients or business model, or highlight one of your case studies in a speech or webinar.

The big tech players have analyst relations departments to keep the briefing machine well-oiled. Yet a surprising number of start-ups and even well-established firms are unfamiliar with the briefing process. So herewith, some insider tips to get the most out of this very important component of a communications strategy process.

In the three and a half years since I joined the Altimeter Group, I've conducted hundreds of briefings with companies large and small, all active in digital marketing, advertising, and media. My Fridays are pretty much reserved for briefings. Briefing calls are scheduled from morning to night, generally starting in Europe and ending somewhere in Silicon Valley. We all limit briefings to 30 minutes to keep them on-topic, and almost never conduct them in person. Most companies requesting briefings ask to do them on site, but travel time is a luxury. It would radically curtail the number of companies with whom we're able to talk.

At Altimeter, we have a system for sharing tagged, cloud-based briefing notes that puts all briefing information at the fingertips of all the company's analysts and researchers. That makes our jobs easier when we're trying to find information on specific types of companies or business, and benefits the companies we speak with, too. They're made more visible to more people.

The above illustrates the value exchange of a briefing. Yet compared with the hundreds, if not thousands, of briefings I've conducted as both a journalist and editor, I'm too often disappointed at how many companies that brief me now that I'm an analyst fail to take full advantage of an opportunity that could benefit us both.

Some suggestions for getting the most out of an analyst briefing.

▶ **Half an hour goes quickly.** I begin every call by telling callers at exactly what time I have a hard stop. Please don't be late. Don't focus on the information available on your website. I've already read it. Too many briefings end with revealing the really new and compelling idea two minutes before our call ends and the next call must begin. Don't bury the lede.

▶ **Five executives on a call are at least three too many.** Again, those 30 minutes elapse quickly. Everyone wants the opportunity to talk. This results in too much noise and very little signal.

▶ **Provide names, titles, and email addresses of who will be on the call — in advance.** We can look up their bios and LinkedIn profiles. This saves a ton of time on intros, and allows me to prepare better, more focused questions. PR people, take particular note. If your name is on the call invitation, but not your client's, I won't dial in.

- **Provide any deck, presentation materials, or online meeting URL at least one day in advance.** The sheer number of companies that send presentation materials literally seconds before (sometimes, during) a briefing is Pet Peeve No. 1. A company did this last Friday via a service that required me to establish, then verify, a new user account in order to download their materials. It's unfair (not to mention impossible) to ask an analyst to do this in what's often literally a 45-second window between two briefings. Let's both agree to be locked, loaded, and ready to go when our briefing is scheduled to begin.

- **Don't assume we're online for the presentation.** Probably we are. But it's not unheard of to conduct a briefing from an airport gate or at a conference with subpar wifi. So really do send those show-and-tell materials in advance.

- **Please talk clearly and into the phone.** Please talk directly into the phone (not the speakerphone), particularly if one of us is speaking a non-native language. We're trying to understand one another. The analyst is also taking notes.

- **A briefing is not a speech, it's a conversation.** In briefings I far too often can't get a word in edgewise, and I'm a person not known to be shy about piping up. Some executives get on a roll and cannot — will not — be stopped until they've delivered a message from beginning to end. (Most often, they're working from a deck and a bit nervous, which they try to cover by being overly verbose.) A briefing is a presentation, but it's also a conversa-

tion. The analyst has questions, as well as a research agenda. So pause. Make an effort to throw in questions such as: Any questions? Is that clear? Does this relate to any research projects you're working on now? Try to make the briefing even more relevant to the analyst than they hoped it would be when they set it up with you.

- **Listen to us, too.** We analysts make our living as strategic, research-based advisors. We're very well connected and ahead-of-the-curve informed about the industry sectors we microscopically cover. A briefing is hardly an advisory session, but we may well make an observation, comparison, or remark that could serve you well. Listen for those nuggets.

- **Go through the proper channels.** Every day I send over a dozen canned responses to the briefing requests I receive personally from companies and PRs alike. I won't accept an emailed request for very good reasons. Like most analyst firms, we have a briefing request form that is designed to capture the information we need to determine if we'll accept a briefing. Moreover, the form alerts all my analyst and researcher colleagues to the opportunity, so one briefing (if accepted) potentially goes much further inside the company. It also greatly streamlines the scheduling process on our side.

That's it from me. What about companies out there that are veterans of analyst briefings? How can we make briefings easier, better and more valuable for you?

The Ripple Effect
of Analyst Relations

Suyog Shetty

'How many deals can you help us win?'

'We have already invested in all the marquee analyst firms, when do we start seeing tangible returns?'

'Can you ask which Fortune 500 firms are being advised?'

These are possibly some of the predominantly asked statements directed to AR professionals by C level (and sometimes the non C level executives). The very fact that these queries are asked, reflects how powerful an audience AR execs deal with every day. And conversely, the subtle fact indicates how little Leadership teams realize the way one collaborates with Analysts.

The beauty is – not just multi-million dollar deal wins, but AR also makes a huge positive impact to the Brand equity of a firm. It's imperative for AR teams to articulate this repeatedly with their leadership, as well as provide them tangible insights on how this role through various platforms is one of the most powerful constituents of Sales and Marketing, equivalently.

Every business service is set up with clear and explicit objective of creating revenues. Evidently, all efforts undertaken for such initiatives have to ensure there is a return in the short or long term. Similarly, various facets of marketing in technology bring about enormous amount of exposure which are tangible, as well as drive home the point on effectiveness of the brand, and why a customer should choose a service provider.

The challenge very often is, several initiatives do not bring you a quick fix result. The gestation period runs into quarters, years as well. Engaging with Analysts is an effort which goes beyond the text book definition of establishing and strengthening relationships. Every touch point needs to be thought through, and not just as an activity where you tick the check boxes.

Doing X number of Briefings, Inquiries and the all-time popular term 'face to face meets' have been the de facto way of justifying to the bosses that this is how it's to be done. Ironically, several leaders also believe buying subscriptions is a straight shot to ensuring a seat on the front row in various reports.

Faring in the marquees

The acknowledged truth of how one performs in major research reports is the pivot to drive several of the firm's efforts. Garnering the resources, and being inclusive in the approach enables significantly for all key leaders to arrange the necessary set of material and importantly the enthusiasm to sustain. This goes much beyond the pipeline – it has the ripple effect by reaching not just buyers, but also peers, media, industry observers who now play a huge and significant role from hereon.

Clearly, AR professionals have to pretty much organize and manage this as a *movement*!

Agreed that one of the most critical benchmarks is evaluating how strongly efforts have resulted in building a pipeline, and subsequently a win. Once the direction of getting the messaging is in place, buyers don't hesitate to have you included in their shortlist – and similarly analysts too would prefer to include you in the short list.

Strengthen the pipe, don't just build

Several myopic approaches are undertaken with the single objective to 'pamper' several analysts, without spending an equivalent amount of time on quality of conversations. Various mid-level managers get excited (and rightly so) with the fact of getting an opportunity to engage with this audience. This excitement can at times get delirious too!

Funnily, several leaders know when to and when not to engage with a customer. How to position, what should be the posture, who should lead the discussion, who should address critical queries and so on are set in place before meeting customers. But, somehow miss the point that an Analyst too is a customer. Fortunately, several firms do acknowledge and appreciate the methods

to be undertaken and prepare more than adequately before planning a critical engagement. Some make mistakes, assuming a phone conversation does not require significant prep which boomerangs over the course of time. Understanding the trends in the industry, narrating what customers are looking for, how they are acknowledging their limitations – and then how the service provider steps in to hand hold, guide and helps them to choose the right fit of platforms, technologies, partnerships to grow – help get across the message to the analysts.

How to work with the Ecosystem

Ensuring the buy-in effectively percolates from the top remains critical. Once the Leadership determines how and what are the parameters that play a significant role in strengthening the relationship, the easier AR professionals find to navigate and have a relevant audience. Some of the leaders bring in such an enormous equity in a discussion, especially those aligned to key verticals the discussions result into an exciting outcome of potentially a research paper or simply an introduction to a buyer. All investments be it money or time give you dividends only because the efforts has been thought through.

With myriad platforms that now demanding attention across twitter/ LinkedIn, many buyers too look for insights that can help them quickly adapt to their needs. Not just platforms, but also the ability to deliver to the end customer successfully and seamlessly. Imagine, such a huge rigmarole gets eliminated by plainly sharing your views and getting across the message directly.

One team or one AR member can move a mountain, however to sustain at a steady pace requires consistent support across all levels and in chorus, to get the desired results!

"I will do it myself." – Why 'Trial and Error' is a Bad Idea in Analyst Relations

*I*f you think back on the many occasions when you've heard this phrase, or for that matter used it yourself – how many times has it been a good idea to give it a try yourself first? Trying something implies that there is the potential to try again if the first attempt fails, or where it is possible to get professional help to get something done after trying once it becomes clear that it isn't something that can be done "on your own".

There are some occasions where trying is certainly a valid option. You can try to cook your dinner and if it fails you can still order a pizza. But trying to fix the brakes on your car might not be such a good idea if you don't exactly know what you are doing.

When it comes to running your business it is in most cases not such a good idea to rely on trying. This is probably one of the reasons why you have job interviews and do your due diligence when you hire someone to work for your company. You want to be sure that the person you are hiring is qualified and experienced enough to get the job done properly.

So how come there are so many people willing to take on the risks involved in engaging external "influencers" on their own without any previous idea of how to get things done?

I am not saying that getting analyst relations wrong is going to threaten your life or the very existence of your company, but it is certainly an important part of building your brand and shaping the perception of your company in the market. So you should better be sure how to get things right.

As in most cases involving interpersonal relationships it is the first impression that counts the most. You probably would not consider sending a junior inexperienced sales rep to an important client. So how come you are willing to approach the handful of relevant analysts for your technology niche without making 100% sure that you understand how the game is played?

I have listened in, and helped prepare dozens of vendor presentations and analyst meetings. It is fair to say that the range of professionalism I have seen varies greatly. Chances are that the analyst you are talking to is covering a large number of vendors and has listened to a huge number of companies trying to "sell" the superiority of their solution. Part of that sales process is also the level of professionalism you are showing in the way you engage with the analyst community.

So if you are willing to compete with your competition in the field of analyst relations, make sure that you are well prepared and have all the tools at hand to win the game. *Trying* to get it right will not be enough when you are competing on a global level and when messing things up might mean that you won't get a second chance to fix things.

Analyst Consulting Days: The Top 4 Reasons Why

*A*nalyst consulting days (aka SAS or strategic advisory service in *Gartnerese*) have a high risk/reward profile for vendor analyst relations (AR) teams. We often receive questions from AR practitioners asking why AR would want to spend the money on an analyst consulting day.

It is important to remember that building strong analyst relationships requires a mix of interaction types. You cannot achieve your objectives using only briefings and inquiry. Consulting days can have significant benefits when done correctly. Because there are different reasons for purchasing analyst consulting days from the firms, vendors need to clarify the goals they want to

pursue through buying consulting days. The shotgun approach of "we'll just throw some more money at them by buying consulting time" rarely succeeds in genuinely increasing an analyst's positive perception of a vendor.

The various reasons why vendors choose to do consulting days vary in real value:

▸ Building stronger relationships with your key analysts can rate as high value when done correctly

▸ To review strategy and product direction or to provide a deep dive style uninterrupted briefing can rate as high value when carefully planned – or be a total waste of resources if not well executed

- Using a consulting day to provide a high profile speaker for an extended marketing event can motivate attendees to better understand the market and be coupled with executive relationship building to produce high value.
- A product-related consulting day done with the product groups can strengthen AR's position within the organisations, build credibility with both company executives and analysts, and improve the product group's understanding of the analysts. You might even be able to get them to pick up the tab.

It is also important to note that analyst consulting days are never effective as:

- A method for gathering market and customer intelligence
- A replacement for a well-planned briefing
- A bribe to the analyst to get them to change their minds.

If executed properly, analyst consulting days can provide the information and executive access that can help change an analyst's opinion, especially when combined with other interactions over time. However, merely writing a check for the consulting day fee is not an instant and easy way to change an opinion. Unfortunately, there is no silver bullet for changing an analyst's opinion.

Kea Company Advice:

- Consulting days should have clearly articulated objectives
- AR teams should carefully review the reasons for buying an analyst consulting day
- Effective consulting days are the result of good planning and appropriate use of resources
- If not initiated by AR, teams should tactfully probe the motivation of an executive or product manager who is requesting an analyst consulting day. If it appears the requester thinks that the day can be a "bribe" then AR needs to educate the requester that this is inappropriate

Bottom Line: Kea Company strongly recommends that vendors determine their goals before they buy analyst consulting days. While a mixture of the goals is certainly possible, being clear about what you are after can lead to more valuable results. In each case, the vendor should also consider whether pursuing other options would achieve the same or better results. Once a consulting day is chosen it is critical to apply appropriate resources to planning and execution. High value consults don't just happen.

AR Classics:
Get Ahead Of Analysts:
The Murphy Approach

Efrem Mallach Ph.D.

For several years in the 1990s I shared a household with an old golden retriever named Murphy. Murphy had ESP. He'd know exactly where one of us would want to be in five minutes. He would position himself right there, in the way. It didn't matter if the place was the refrigerator, the best chair to watch TV, or the bathroom door. Wherever it was, there was Murphy—ahead of us – where he knew he would get our love and attention.

Murphy has passed on to the land of eternal bones to chew on and grass to romp through. But one of his lessons lives on: if you want to be effective in analyst relations, figure out where the analysts you support will want to go, and get there ahead of them.

That's easy to say, of course. But, speaking practically, how can you do this? If you don't have Murphy's psychic abilities, how can you read an analyst's mind?

Fortunately, you don't need ESP to find out where an analyst will want to be. You may not always be able to position him or her at the refrigerator or TV set, but analysts' professional lives are easier to figure out. The key factor is *how the analyst's business works*.

There are four basic business modes. Many analysts work in more than one from time to time but most tend to emphasise one or two of them. These modes may apply to a firm as a whole or, at a large firm, on an analyst-by-analyst basis. These basic business modes, and how you should treat analysts in each mode, are:

Scheduled

This applies to firms who analyze and forecast market shares and volumes. They follow a quarterly or annual cycle. They need specific information at a certain point during their cycle. Earlier, it's not available. Later, it's too late.

Find out what they need and when in the quarter (or year) they need it. Start collecting it before then, so it can be ready by their deadline without creating a rush situation in your company.

Planned

These firms offer subscribers a series of (usually monthly) reports. They plan their research calendar months in advance. Some firms publicize it as a selling point for potential clients. Others see it as a competitive issue, and disclose upcoming topics only when it's too late for others to copy the idea.

Call these firms every six weeks or so and ask "Do you have any upcoming reports where I can start collecting information for you?" Offering meetings with your firm's technical and marketing staff is also useful.

Event-Driven

These firms report on industry events, analyzing new products and services, discussing executives' strategic pronouncements and who's moving up or down. They can't tell you what they'll report on next month because they don't know what you (or any other vendor) will do next month. You, however, do know, at least for your firm.

Pre-briefings (under suitable non-disclosure agreements, sometimes called embargos) are called for here. Let them get a head start on analyzing and reporting your news, so they can get answers to their questions and do it justice when the press calls them.

Client-Driven

These firms or analysts operate more as consultants. In some cases they're hard to tell from any other consultant. In others, they simple apply their firm's existing research to individual clients' needs. In either case, they won't know what they'll be asked about until the client asks.

Keep them informed at a background level of what your company is doing, what exciting new capabilities it has, and how they can get more information quickly when they need it.

The really good news is that *analysts will tell you which mode applies most strongly to their work*. All you have to do is ask! They're happy to tell you, with as many specifics as they can possibly provide. And it shows you care.

Asking also prevents you from making embarrassing mistakes that may hurt your relationship with them. For example, suppose you ask an event-driven analyst "Are you working on anything we can start collecting information on?" The most likely response is "We don't work that way here. Are you about to announce anything? If you are, that's what I'm working on, so tell me." Your question, while fully appropriate for an analyst who works in planned mode, accomplished nothing. Ask it once, and you haven't done much damage. Ask it twice, and you prove that (a) you don't understand that analyst's business, and (b) you weren't paying attention the first time.

Once you ask, though, your job's not done. You have to keep the information and use the information. Enter it into your analyst database and refer to it when you make your regular "keep in touch" calls. For analysts who work in scheduled mode, enter key dates on your calendar or tickler file. For those who work in client-driven mode, make sure you have experts on relevant topics lined up so they can swing into action on short notice. For the event-driven analysts, be sure the non-disclosure agreements are ready to be signed and the materials are ready for them the minute their signature is on the paper. If you can do this, Murphy would be proud of you.

Create a New Market Category by Courting Analysts Your Customers Respect

Anthony Kennada

Marketing is by far the most complex organization within a business. The same individuals tasked with building brand standards and designing websites are also architects of intricate demand generation programs to drive lead flow to the sales team. Often these left-brained / right-brained activities are at odds with one another, which eventually leads to specialization within the team.

But as the VP Marketing building a new category of software, your job is to be great at both! In fact, a third dimension of activities exists that focus on your ability to influence, or story-tell with conviction and confidence. Nowhere is that skill set more important than in your efforts leading an Analyst Relations or "AR" strategy.

Analysts are key to new category definition.

When creating new market categories, it's your job to build a framework around the needs and pains of this market. Some of that outcome is realized through your content marketing efforts. But in order for a new category to *actually* become a new category, you need trusted third-party validation, or what I call a "sphere of influence" to back your claims.

Customers are a major part of a company's sphere of influence. In another post, I went into great detail on this very subject, explaining how Customer Success is the new Marketing. But beyond your install base, the other strategic pillar to your company's sphere of influence is the analyst community that your potential customers are engaged with.

Analysts by nature are vendor-neutral and typically have a deep Rolodex of contacts who actively listen to their perspective. Their name alone often carries a certain distinction that connotes authority. When operating in a new market, building those key relationships can mean the difference between a category leader and follower. Understanding how to influence these folks requires comprehending the distinctions of each.

Different Types of Analysts.

Each market will have different nuances based on maturity and vertical, however there are typically three types of analysts that emerge throughout the lifecycle of your AR program:

1. The Subject Matter Expert. Also regarded as a "thought leader", Subject Matter Experts are independent bloggers or advocates who have developed some type of following that garners attention. They typically are not employed by any competitors and are seen as first-movers in building community around the pains and needs of your market. You would likely engage with these individuals to market through them and to their following, as they typically will not charge you for an engagement. Rather, they are more focused on growing their own sphere of influence, and rising to the top as an independent, vendor-neutral player in the space.

2. The Super Consultant. Similar to a Subject Matter Expert, Super Consultants are independents that have gained notoriety in your young market. Unlike them, however, they will charge you for their services. These are the individuals who offer consulting services for speaking engagements, content partnerships, and other programs that focus far beyond distribution. You may consider working with Super Consultants to add credibility to your cause, especially when the market has yet to tip towards our next class of analysts.

3. The Majors. These are the "tier-one" corporations who have built withstanding businesses on offering trusted advice to your potential customers. If you work in technology, you are no stranger to brands like Gartner, Forrester, and IDC. Working with any one of The Majors means fighting for the support of the loudest voices in your category. This effort is usually pretty costly, however, an incredibly important endeavor that requires early and frequent investment in order to bear fruit.

Approaching an analyst relationship. You will almost certainly encounter each type of analyst in your efforts to market a new category. Your ability to influence will set you apart, but as will your ability to create a steady drumbeat and cadence of check-ins with analysts across all types that are covering your market. Here are a few reasons to engage with an analyst:

Upcoming product release. Keeping the analyst community up to speed on your latest product innovation will help reinforce your relevance in the space. You likely did not need to sell them on the pain, but with each release, you are selling them on why your product is the undisputed solution to address that pain.

Customer case studies. What better way to strengthen your market leadership than by offering paying (and happy) customers to speak to their ROI with your solution? Analysts will typically appreciate the chance to speak with customers, especially when the particular case study maps to their field of research.

Co-marketing opportunities. If you're able to find an analyst who buys into your vision for the market, they will generally surface opportunities to partner on content efforts. These projects are typically high-value (albeit expensive in The Majors) and will differentiate your content campaigns with critical third-party validation. You'll find that this investment will often produce better results than standard content campaigns and will further the perception of your market leadership.

Just because. It's not uncommon for new markets to operate at the edges of existing ones. This means that although a well-known analyst firm may not have a research agenda that correlates *directly* to your category, they certainly have analysts covering tangential categories who are worthy of briefing. By using any of the tactics above, it's your regular check-ins with these indirect analysts that can often convert to direct coverage.

Every marketer may have a different bias when it comes to engaging with analysts, but when building a new category, their authority and influence can support your thought leadership efforts beyond any other program. Invest early and often, and you'll be sure to see the impact that analysts can make on both your market leadership, and ultimately, pipeline of prospects.

$$= \sqrt[n]{4^n +}$$

$$= \sqrt[n]{6^n + 7^n +}$$

$$= \frac{n \cdot \sin(2n)}{(3n - 1)^2}$$

$$\cos(4n)$$

Crunching the Numbers –
Behind the Scenes
of an Analyst Briefing Campaign

*I*t is quite easy to talk about the qualitative aspects of analyst relations, but when it comes down to the numbers, things tend to get more confusing. Measuring has become a holy grail of business operations and a lot of times things that can't be measured in terms of ROI get discarded quite quickly. For this reason a lot of effort has been put into finding ways to measure the impact of analyst relations on the success of the business. By tracking the number of leads and deals generated or influenced by analysts and by tracking the number of analysts' mentions a company gets in research publications, the media or at public speaking events most vendors have by now come to understanding the value of analyst relations for the business. Looking at the individual analyst this could mean the following: A typical research report (e. g. a Magic Quadrant) from a major analyst firm easily attracts thousands of readers throughout the year it is published in. At the same time it is not uncommon for an analyst to have around 500 inquiry calls per year with a significant portion of these focusing on vendor/product selection related topics. On top of this the analyst will probably write a blog, tweet, engage in social media, give interviews to the media and will speak at several events throughout a year. By adding up these numbers **the**

potential exposure for a vendor created by a single analyst can easily add-up to several thousand contact points with relevant prospects.

But what about the effort that has to be put into reaching the right analysts? When we are talking about ROI we often forget to thoroughly analyze the 'Invest' part of the equation. In many cases the executive at a vendors presenting in the briefing only sees the time spent talking to the analysts but has no understanding of the time and effort required to identify and engage the relevant analysts before a briefing can take place. Obviously this is not all that is required to make a successful briefing happen but for this post I will disregard the strategy planning and content creation which of course is a major part of any analyst relations program. At Kea Company we initiate, plan, organize and execute several hundred briefings each year. This gives us a unique understanding of the logistics that are happening behind the scenes of an analyst briefing campaign.

Sometimes **finding the right analysts to talk to can be like searching for the needle in the haystack**: There are about 10.000 IT analysts in roughly 800 analyst firms focusing on more than a hundred different technology areas and verticals. So narrowing down the field can be quite a daunting challenge. What I did for this blog is to look at our Analyst Tracking System to get some solid numbers based on our real world experience. Of course these numbers are only averages and there is quite a wide spread around this average depending on technology area or vendor focus (e. g. regional or vertical). So let's focus on our example vendor 'Average Tech Corp' who is briefing 25 different analysts per year. What does this mean in terms of identifying and engaging analysts before this can happen? First of all you have to do a search (e. g. via the internet by visiting all the analyst firms' websites) to do an initial screening and create a pool of potentially relevant analysts. For 'Average Tech Corp' this means he ends up with 400 analysts who seem to have some connection to the topics which are relevant for this vendor. After a more in-depth session spent on reading the bios of these analysts and by taking a look at their focus areas this field gets narrowed down to 200 analysts. A more in-depth screening (e. g. by reading their blogs, browsing through their recently published research and by studying their research agenda) narrows down the field to 100 analysts who are relevant for 'Average Tech Corp'. Full of enthusiasm the Analyst Relations pro at 'Average Tech Corp' reaches out to each of these analysts with a tailored briefing request which highlights the relevance of 'Average Tech Corp' for this particular analyst. After exchanging some more emails and finding out that some of the analysts have changed focus, left the company or are about to retire next week he ends up with 25 agreed briefings for 'Average Tech Corp'.

This effort probably took about 400 hours and required some prior knowledge of the analyst space and as mentioned doesn't include the content and strategy side of the analyst relations program. Also providing feedback and input for research publications requires additional time and effort. **So is it all worth it? Yes, definitely**: Circling back to the beginning of this post: Each analyst can result in more than 10.000 qualified contacts with your target audience. So the 25 analyst briefings have the potential to greatly increase your marketreach making analyst relations one of the most efficient tools in the marketing mix of a technology vendor.

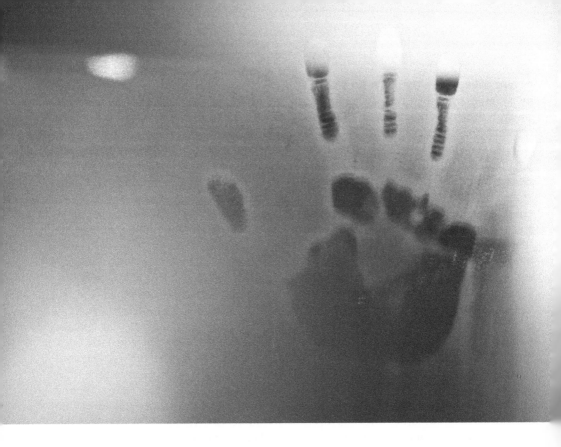

Killer products don't sell

Of course they do. Didn't we just manage to convince the first 50 customers to buy our solution? Yes, you did. But now ask yourself what the reasons for closing those deals were. What were the parameters involved in getting your customers to evaluate the products in the first place?

In many cases a product convincing a customer to buy it is only the last step in a long row of interactions. For your company to be short listed and considered for a proof of concept workshop or product trial your will have to pass many gates along the way. First of all you will have to get some visibility in the market. And yes, those 50 customers will help you spread the word about your solution but usually this kind of **word of mouth marketing runs dry after you have saturated your local market.** It is very hard to fuel your growths outside your comfort zone with purely recommendation driven marketing. There are many reasons for this. First of all your network (and that of your current customers) will be limited to a certain type of connections. This means you will likely be going in circles when it comes to regional markets, verticals or other customer parameters. You can check on this by looking at your current customer base. If you are successful in a specific niche you can leverage this to saturate that niche. **But in the end a niche is a niche and you will need to break out of your niche to fuel your company's growths for the coming years.** One way to do this is to hire people with access to target groups you want to address. But left to their own devices they will still lack the support and credibility needed to successfully sell your solution. This lack of supporting noise is often the reason why sales efforts fail even though you've hired top performers who successfully sold into the same market segment before.

Don't get me wrong, I am pretty sure that your product has some unique features which will let it stand out among the competition. But this is a claim that your potential customers will hear from most of the vendors out there. Even those features that you believe are unique to your solution might be available from some competitor elsewhere (a competitor who is obviously also relying on his "killer product" to do the selling for him – or otherwise you would have heard of him right?). One way to stand out from the competition and to circumvent the issue of "not being one of the big players with a reputation" is by having known and trusted market experts do the branding for you. This includes convincing editors, industry analysts and other thought leaders of the quality and innovation you are bringing to the market. It is much more likely that your customers will make their shortlist decisions based on an unbiased analyst's opinion than on what your / your competitors' sales people suggest. In addition the market reach of those influencers will be much greater than what you can expect to create by yourself in the short term.

It seems to me that the opinion that it only takes a good product to be successful in the market is especially strong in the technology sector. In high-tech markets many companies and solutions are driven by continuous innovation. In addition many of these companies have founders with a technical background who are keen to innovate and improve what they have built. It is very easy for technology start-ups and emerging vendors to fall into this trap. The initial success of their solution in combination with fresh venture capital money on the table make it easy to underestimate the challenges (and costs) of breaking into new markets. So when you are growing your company **please make sure that you give your products the chance to get evaluated by the customer**. Spending all your money on product innovation without doing a good job in sales and marketing won't work. Equally just sending out more sales people and expecting them to generate the trust needed for successful completion of a sale is pretty much doomed. Last but not least doing marketing and generating leads without a proper sales team to follow up on those leads and without a product to fulfil the expectations you have created won't make sense either.

So if you are planning to succeed you should try to integrate your product development, marketing and sales efforts to leverage the synergies and to make sure that you don't create any bottle necks. Influencer Relations with its sub-disciplines of PR, Analyst Relations and social media marketing can help you to align your efforts by not only giving you more visibility in the market, but also by providing a feedback channel and a 3rd party perspective on your products. So if you truly believe that you have a killer product I encourage you to give it the chance to sell itself – not only to your customers but also to those influencers out there who will in the end shape the way your solution and your company is perceived in the market

Pitches Fail Because of Misunderstanding and Distrust

Analysts don't think it's their job to help failing spokespeople. Rather than speak up, analysts will often let executives hang themselves with their own rope. That's the sad story emerging this month, as my colleague Christian and I speak with analysts who look part in the recent Analyst Attitude Survey. Roughly half of the 150 participants in the survey have volunteered for follow-up calls, and they are especially forthcoming in telling us what's going wrong in those stressful pitch meetings when providers come in to update analysts on solutions.

Trustworthiness, market knowledge and transparency are three of the most important things that analysts are looking for. Sadly, they are often lacking.

It might be self-evident that spokespeople should be honest and true when they meet analysts. Analysts are telling us that it's often not the case. They are able to recognise honesty in many ways, and responsiveness is the clue that the most analysts look for first. Spokespeople often use the classic media relations techniques (control – bridge – sell) to block the analysts' interests and divert the conversation back to a prepared recital. This actually harms vendors. On the other hand, discussing analysts' interests shows more than knowledge that providers are respectful, open to questioning and criticism, and prioritise market realities rather than corporate dogma.

Many analysts find that spokespeople come with a presentation that has been reused to the point of boredom. Rolling out a well-worn deck is often seen as an attempt to control the conversation and avoid the serious effort involved in understanding individual analysts' needs. Rather than inform analysts with valuable market insight, they sell the solution to the analyst as if they were a potential buyer or reseller. Rather than specify how customers benefit from solutions to particular business problems, spokespeople bring slides with customer logos and technical diagrams that look anything but unique. One analyst told us that it seems almost taboo to prepare briefings seriously by checking to make sure spokespeople understand the analysts' information needs. Frustratingly, it's clear that there is preparation: Many reported how vendors mine analysts' resumes in order to find commonalities or points for small talk. Very few, however, reported the same effort has been put into anticipating their information needs.

Sadly when some spokespeople do review analysts' work, they might not get the balance right between either accepting or challenging research findings. Not all analysts think the same way. Some want challenge, and others done. Some want focus, and others want breadth. The key to all of this is to understand the analysts. To get a better idea of how to do that, check out Efrem Mallach's book, Win Them Over.

There's no Such Thing as a Free Lunch

*T*he economic theory, and also the lay opinion, that whatever goods and services are provided, they must be paid for by someone – i.e. you don't get something for nothing. The phrase is also known by the acronym of 'There ain't no such thing as a free lunch' – tanstaafl.

What is wrong with this world? Why do people talk nonsense fifty percent of the day? I am clearly fed up with this. I exactly took thirty minutes out of my busy schedule to tell this to you.

For the past twelve months, I have been dealing with Small (very small) and Medium businesses myself. It is always noble to help the people that can use it the most. I know that this is not the easiest business to conquer, but it is my own choice. In those twelve months, I had around a hundred meetings I joined myself to see if it leads to victory. I think I experienced around twenty meetings that had anything to do with a decent education and thoughts about how they wanted to work with others. So for the people who question what I just said; common knowledge on how to behave when you need something and have something to offer in return.

This leaves us with eighty meetings where you can mildly question the request up to where you walk out in fifteen minutes because their boldness is shameless. And mind you, we are clear on the phone before we jump in the car. So why do people behave like this? Why would you treat people like that? Did you miss certain education when you lived back home?

I know one thing for sure. They keep trying because there are still people out there with no self-esteem. You can't tell me that this is normal behaviour. If you would like to receive the help, you should expect to provide something in return. Normally money would be just fine. If you don't like that, don't make the call. Figure it out yourself. If you think it is all to expensive, don't blame others, learn how to use a calculator. There's no such thing as a free lunch.

How to fit to business policies

Bimodal in a digital world: To be or not to be

Anirban Chakraborty

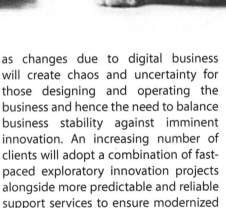

ℛ ecently, there has been a lot of debate on "Bimodal IT" as two of the leading industry analyst firms have proposed diametrically opposite views. Bimodal IT is the practice of managing two separate, coherent modes of IT delivery; one focused on stability and the other on agility.

Mode 1 is traditional and sequential, emphasizing safety and accuracy. Mode 2 is exploratory and nonlinear, emphasizing agility and speed (http://www.gartner.com/it-glossary/bimodal). Gartner suggests such an approach

as changes due to digital business will create chaos and uncertainty for those designing and operating the business and hence the need to balance business stability against imminent innovation. An increasing number of clients will adopt a combination of fast-paced exploratory innovation projects alongside more predictable and reliable support services to ensure modernized and secure IT environments.

On the other hand, Forrester feels that bimodal IT creates two separate groups that work at different speeds on segregated systems. It is fundamentally unable to address customer and enterprise needs for agility. CIOs need a single strategy to accelerate innovation and simplification, not a two-class system that adds more front-end and back-end silos of complexity. It makes no sense to have two groups competing for funding, resources, skills and the business' attention. They feel that bimodal IT will only widen the gulf between the CIO and the business. A unified strategy is needed to engage and energize the C-suite and board. Firms that do not embrace such a unified strategy and continue to hedge with a bimodal strategy will face the additional cost and complexity of running two parallel systems. And without the simplification and modernization of core operational systems in areas like supply chain management and core banking, they will be forced to use manual process workarounds to meet the needs of customers — all of which will drive up costs and hurt margins.

Couple of thoughts on the above approaches:

▸ Most organizations today are still struggling to define what digital means for them; digital transformation requires leadership from the very top as it affects the entire way of working for the organization as well as its clients. In the absence of a clear understanding of what digital means, a bimodal strategy is what would work best wherein fast-paced exploratory projects help the company realize its digital future while it continues to modernize its current IT environment.

▸ There is often no clear ownership of who owns digital. Most of the organizations consider this as a primary barrier to achieving digital transformation. In such a scenario, you have different buyers of IT services like the CIO, CMO and others LOBs. Service providers realize this and are trying to help different buyers in the client organizations via bimodal IT – Mode 1 where the innovation focus is on objectives such as the industrialization and automation of delivery services and processes and the overall modernization of core IT systems. In Mode 2, service providers aim to start small, be agile and take fast action on opportunities, fail fast and adapt.

▸ Legacy IT systems in most organizations resemble more

like noodle soup than a coherent interconnection of systems. One of the core ideas behind digital is to adopt an agile sprint-based approach wherein some specific processes are first taken into consideration and transformed using a "fail fast – learn fast" approach trying than a multi-year overhaul of the entire system. In the meanwhile, one still needs to run existing environments to make sure that clients' needs don't suffer. Hence, the need for incremental change rather than a Big-Bang approach.

▶ As per http://www.computerworld. in/news/why-bimodal-it-kills-your-culture-and-adds-complexity – Bill Ruh, the Chief Digital Officer at GE Digital told CIO.com the problem organizations run into creating bimodal systems is the stigma that the mode 1 group operating back-office systems is slower than the mode 2 unit building digital technologies. Employees may not want to work on mode 1 because of the perception that it is not innovative. This is in line with what Forrester says and retaining talent in Mode 1 will certainly be a challenge with Bimodal IT.

▶ Forrester is right in saying that traditional IT delivery methods can't meet the rising expectations of customers and the increasing speed of innovation. Bimodal IT does not talk about the broader business, process, and organizational changes required to improve customer experience and operational excellence. If organizations can have clear leadership, ownership and budgets for Digital wherein groups don't compete for funding, resources, skills and the business' attention; then a unified strategy is certainly possible. Forrester is right in saying that calls for a complete shift to put customers at the center of technology strategy and to operate as one team.

Overall, there is merit to what both firms say and, if one reads between the lines, one will find that the views are not as diametrically opposite as they would appear and there are points wherein both firms are actually in agreement.

Do You Know Who That Is?

*W*e get the feeling that sales enablement is something that popped up recently in the office of many AR professionals. How is that possible, you might ask yourself. Well, the people that pay your salary are just being informed about what AR does and how it can contribute even more to the company.

Our apologies for that "extra" work (not really).

We like to look at it in a different way; We just saved your job. Informing the analyst firms is only fifty percent of your job today. Please make sure you do understand that things change, also in the world of marketing and influencer relations. I spoke many times about shifting budgets. It happens too often that people wake up when it is already too late. Make preparations. Move to the front before your budget holder does. Make sure you provide them with ideas that other parts of the organisation can benefit from.

Just a quick suggestion from Kea Company: make twenty questions. Of course, those questions should be AR-related. Ask people if they know companies like Gartner or Bloor Research. Also ask them if they are aware of your company showing up in research, written by X firms and if they would use it for selling to new clients. Now start to push every week a one-page sheet to the sales force with the information they can do something with. Try this for about ten weeks. Evaluate and ask

the same twenty questions again. I bet you they can all answer them by now. The real creative part I'll leave to you, but if you need help you know of course where to find us.

The point being awareness. This will not be accomplished by hiding behind doing vendor briefings or making powerpoint slides nobody cares about. They won't see the benefit that the senior management team will see. But that other fifty percent of your time you can show the value to the man and women of the salesforce. Make fans and position AR as a true added value to your total organisation, not only your shareholders.

How Tech Providers Can Get Value from Gartner (and other Analysts)

Hank Barnes

One of the most common questions I get when talking to prospective and existing Gartner clients (note: is: how can we get the most value from a Gartner relationship? Here are some other thoughts that I typically share. Many of them are applicable to any industry analyst, or influencer, you might work with. This takes the perspective of a client relationship, where you have access to connect with analysts for inquiries on a variety of topics, not just briefings.

Understand their Role and Audience and Mission

Not all analysts have the same focus and audience. Most people in Analyst Relations understand this, but as you get broader in the organization, they may not.

The first thing to do is understand, and communicate, the analyst's audience, purpose, and coverage. What is their coverage area and what audience to they focus on. At Gartner, most of the attention and awareness is around our End User Analysts who cover various technology areas. Their mission is clear–help IT Buyers make better purchase decisions. If you are a vendor (we call them providers) you can interact with these analysts, but its important to remember their focus is buyer success.

Gartner also has a large group of analysts that focus on providers (T&SP). Our mission (I'm part of that team) is to help providers grow faster. We spend our time helping providers understand market forecasts, dynamics and opportunities, while also advising on go-to-market strategies. Depending on coverage area, many T&SP analysts also advise buyers, but their perspective is driven around overall market dynamics.

Once you have that perspective you can set your priorities for analyst interactions, determining if the goal is influence or improvement.

TACTICS TO INCREASE INFLUENCE

▶ ***Engage, Don't Battle, to Increase Influence***

If the goal is influence, think collaborative engagement vs. arguing over who is right. Argumentative approaches have an impact that goes beyond the core truth of the argument as it creates more personal emotions. If you disagree with an analyst opinion, ask them what they see in the market that drove that opinion. Then point out the things you are seeing–with examples–to share your point of view. If you agree, acknowledge that and talk about other similar thoughts that might expand the discussion. Finding ways to help analysts broaden their perspective on what is happening in their technology sector, or things they should be looking for, is a very effective strategy when done in a collaborative manner.

▶ ***Ask Pointed Questions***

As you develop a collaborative relationship with your key analysts, you've earned the ability to ask direct questions that are key to analyst relations strategies. If you think you

should have been mentioned in a report and were not, ask why. Ask

what else you need to share with the analyst for them to more completely understand your product or company. Finally, and perhaps most importantly, ask them in what situations do they recommend your firm when IT buyers come to them looking for suggestions. You can ask these questions at any time, but I've found the dialog is much more productive and engaging once you've strengthened the relationship.

▶ ***Encourage Prospective Clients to Call***

This is an important, and often overlooked tactic. If you like the way the analyst describes the situations when they recommend you (i.e. it aligns with your positioning and messaging), then encourage your prospective clients (who also have a Gartner relationship) to contact the analyst. Then, let the analyst know who will be calling and why. This approach is great for a couple of reasons. First, while you can't participate or control the conversation, you need to remember that the prospect will probably leverage Gartner research or inquiries anyway. Second, it displays a level of confidence that your prospects should find reassuring. (Note: This tactic should apply to any analyst firm your work with–not just Gartner)

TACTICS TO DRIVE IMPROVEMENT

▸ *Use the Research*

Our research can be of much more value than just evaluating where you fall in a Magic Quadrant. Use Gartner Research as one the inputs to your product strategies (along with customer feedback, competitive information, and win/loss data). Use forecasts to help choose new markets to enter. If you do use research in your efforts, tell the author about it. Analysts love to hear how their research helps readers.

▸ *Treat as Team Members*

This is particularly true for T&SP analysts, but you should view us as advisors that are an extension of your teams (in my case–marketing)–albeit totally independent As you develop strategies, you can work with us to refine your plans. Then as you produce outputs, we can review them prior to finalization. We regularly review presentations, marketing campaigns, collateral, and more–providing an external voice that can often find things that were missed in internal reviews.

WORST PRACTICES

While the above outlined some best practices (and in some cases highlighted things not to do), there are some worst practices that I have seen and hear about regularly (both in my time at Gartner and throughout the years when I was on the other side of the table).

Briefing Based Strategy Days – Strategy days are a great opportunity for deep analyst engagement. The focus of these should be improvement, with the dialog that results creating positive influence opportunities. That does not always happen. The ideal agenda should be a mix of discussions led by you and the Gartner analyst(s)–roughly a 50/50 split–with lots of time for interaction. This creates a lot of positive energy. Unfortunately, I've worked at places where strategy days were treated as extended briefing opportunities–where the provider content dominated the agenda–leaving little time for engaging discussion. Analysts leave these meetings feeling discouraged and frustrated.

Not Engaging Until Things are "Perfect" – While this strategy might be almost okay (nothing is ever perfect though) for a briefing, it makes no sense to do this for inquiries. Engage when you have a clear idea of what you want to discuss and have some material or ideas (strawman or better) to share. If you wait for perfection, you are indirectly telling the analyst that their opinion does not matter.

All About the Product – Many firms fall in love with their technology and spend all their time with analysts talking about it. This could be one of the biggest and most common mistakes. Analysts have to help end users make better buying decisions, and many other factors, particularly information about your customers, your company and why you can be trusted and have staying power are equally, and sometimes more, important. Make sure you tell the whole story about why IT buyers should choose your firm and product.

Content is Key! –
Leveraging Influencer
Marketing
To Gain Market Mindshare

*I*n a world that is dominated by "push-advertising" and that includes an overwhelming choice of products and services that need to be evaluated by the buyer, it is increasingly hard to find ways to stand out from the crowd. According to many studies we are now facing a world that is so saturated with advertising that many companies are seeing diminishing returns on their traditional marketing efforts.

More often than not it is consumer generated content that gets favored by the readers when it comes to making buying decisions. In this context however, the term 'consumer generated' refers not only to peer reviews and end-user product evaluations but has to be seen in a broader context. Any form of content that is not (obviously) paid for and distributed by the business itself gets a bonus when it comes to trustworthiness.

But creating original content is only one side of the problem: With many channels – both traditional ones like TV, news magazines and post mailings and new ones like blogs, social media groups and peer networks – competing for the attention of the individual, it is equally important to choose the right channels for every kind of content to ensure that your message is heard.

The purpose of influencer relations in this context is to (in part) 'outsource' the responsibility for content creation and managing the communication channel to those individuals that are most influential in any given channel. The important part is to provide the facts and 'building blocks' needed to create relevant content featuring your business, products and services, thus significantly increasing your market reach and brand awareness. By establishing the right relationships with the relevant influencers (like business analysts, editors and bloggers) you can get the world to know what your business is about.

But finding out how to leverage the potential of influencer relations for maximum impact is a complex challenge. For this reason influencer relations agencies play a critical role in establishing the relationships to the influencers and are key to the success of the entire marketing mix. The reason for this is that influencer relations agencies focus both on creating original content and at the same time act as moderators and facilitators in the distribution process. By defining and managing the channels (e. g. public relations, social media or analyst relations) and deciding what type of content to make available to which channel and influencer, they take a central position in creating market mindshare for a brand.

Ultimately content marketing, supported by the right type and quality of content and distributed by the right influencers, will be a powerful marketing tool for any business.

When Your Company Takes Out Your Favorite Analyst

Peggy O'Neill

*I*t happens to the best of us. Your analyst relations program is humming along nicely – your analysts are behaving, your internal constituents under control – when one day, wham! You get a call from one of your SVPs sharing some exciting news! Joe Analyst, one of your company's key advocates, has now joined your company.

AR managers will inevitably grapple with this scenario as analysts migrate to vendors often. Informatica took out two high profile analysts last year and I've experienced this at previous employers too. AR managers can expect certain behaviors when an analyst who used to cover your company comes inside, so your best bet is to prepare for when that day hits and take full advantage of the opportunity.

Surprise! You'll be the Last to Know

Odds are good this will come as a surprise. Most analysts explicitly request confidentiality and ask that AR (and anyone else not directly part of the recruiting process) not be told of interviews in case things don't work out. That's fair – when dealing with personnel issues, people should and need to be discreet.

So your SVP will be all smiles and trying to feed you a line such as, "It's great that we got Joe Analyst to join our team! He's so smart! Now we don't have to settle for measly inquiry or expensive consulting to tap his knowledge."

Keep in mind that this is nearly always an analyst who is bullish on your company. Chances are you have had repeated interactions with this analyst for some time. As we know, analysts feel more comfortable recommending your company when they really understand it. Unfortunately your company did too good a job – your analyst has now fallen in love to the point of wanting to take part in the journey.

Make the Most Out of Your Response to the Hiring Exec

Your first reaction should be an unexpected one. Your SVP is expecting you to react positively to his or her brilliant hire. Indulge in some dramatic eye rolling, growl at your exec, and point out that while he has just added to his brain trust, he has taken out a positive analyst and created more work for you personally. Seize the opportunity to milk this. Slap your hand to your forehead and sarcastically suggest that next time he wants an analyst, to please consult his AR expert. Share how you would preferably steer him to a negative analyst. Better to recruit a critical analyst who wants to fix things than an analyst who agrees with your company's strengths. Taking out a negative analyst does more to advance the AR cause than leaving a gaping hole in your positive analyst line up.

After your SVP finishes chuckling and concedes you have a clever idea for future analyst hires, ask him for some impressive resumes. Explain that you need to see if you can help refer someone positive in that open position your company just created. You'll need to find another analyst to replace the one you lost and, if you can pull it off, helping someone get

placed is the best way to recruit another groupie. This is a great opportunity for your SVP to see you adjusting rapidly and strategically to a challenging event.

You'll also need to apologize to your analyst firm for taking out a good analyst and do your best to ingratiate yourself with the hiring manager as you'll be sending resumes his or her way. And, of course, you're not allowed to complain about coverage gaps, delayed reports, long inquiry turnarounds for a few months at least.

The Inside Conversation with Your Ex-Analyst and New Colleague

Now it's time to have a chat with your new colleague. Start by reminding him or her that you're likely the only person in the company not happy about their arrival, and baldly point out how his or her departure has now created uncertainty and more work in your world. Again, milk this for all its worth. Then ask for your new colleague's help and shift the conversation to a debrief. What did his former employer really think of us? Who are the best analysts to cultivate, whose star is on the rise and who is checking out? Get your former analyst to conduct a debrief on behind-the-scenes politics – of course while they continue to maintain confidentiality. The analyst is usually happy to dish and you've created a shift in the relationship dynamic, demonstrating to the former analyst you're both now on the same team. This accelerates the indoctrination process while you lay the foundation for an effective relationship with your new colleague.

Without a doubt, your former analyst is going to ask about passwords. By nature analysts are info junkies and they've been accustomed to having unlimited access to their own research, so it may come as a shock that you don't have a password ready for them. Every company manages password distribution and AR budgets differently, so there's no universal rule of thumb here. However, analyst relations should be an influencing function first, and a market research function second. If you have a scanty AR budget, you shouldn't be giving passwords willy-nilly to people, even if they really appreciate them (the way a former analyst will). Passwords funded by AR should be for spokespeople and others who interact regularly with the analyst community. Don't make a special exception for your new colleague just because he's a former analyst. People who want passwords for research to do their jobs need to get their managers to fund seats, not AR.

In addition to the password discussion, early on you'll want to discuss rules of engagement – how to leverage their relationships without undermining your authority. Don't try to issue any dumb edicts such as they're not allowed to interact with their former colleagues whom they've known for years. You'll just come across as an insecure control freak. Simply remind your new colleague you're on the same team and routine analyst requests need to be sent to you so that his former colleagues don't mistake his new role for being AR. Point out there will be opportunities to use him as a diplomat, a spy, or a cop. With his relationships and knowledge, you could use him as a back channel to socialize new things or float trial balloons. He's now an additional intelligence source as his old colleagues may divulge stuff to him unofficially. And the two of you can play good cop and bad cop with his old firm now that he's part of your team.

Also, an annoying dynamic may erupt if your analyst has an interest in AR. Internal people may go to him for AR advice or your former analyst may insert himself into AR matters. If you find this happening too frequently with no abatement, you need to nip this in the bud by asking if he plans a career change and has ambitions to transfer to your group. You also need to do some soul searching and ask why your internal people are turning to him as an expert and not you.

Look at the Positives

On the plus side, you now have a new partner who can help educate others about how to truly leverage analysts. And you now have a polished spokesperson who can speak effectively to your analysts. You may get a new needy constituent, but they really do understand how to leverage market research. The bad news is that you'll be asked for lots of reports and inquiries.

Bottom line: if you manage the transition well, you'll experience a burst of activity initially but then your former analyst will settle into his job and you've gained an internal ally who helps you advance the AR cause.

This blog is dedicated to my colleagues Julie Lockner and Rob Karel, who have been a pain and a delight to work with. Peggy O'Neill is Director of Analyst Relations at Informatica. Any analysts positively disposed toward Informatica are discouraged from applying for employment.

Leverage

How to benefit from working with analysts

Filtering the Noise: Analyst Relations As An Intelligence Gathering System

Christopher Manfredi

*Communications
without intelligence
is noise; Intelligence
without communications
is irrelevant.*

– Gen Alfred Gray, USMC

The very first United States intelligence unit was the Office of Naval Intelligence (ONI), created in 1882. While the US had already had its hands in spy workings, from George Washington's desire to create a clandestine area in the Secret Service following his use of spies during the Revolutionary War to the numerous reconnaissance missions by both the North and the South of the American Civil War, the ONI went immediately to work gathering up to the minute information on global navies.

This unit that began as just a way to peak into the latest technologies of naval warfare along with some broad foreign knowledge has morphed into the largest intelligence gathering apparatus the world has ever seen. The current intelligence gathering has grown into seventeen governmental agencies to include the Central Intelligence Agency, the Office of National Intelligence and the National Security Agency, of recent fame following its revelations from informant Edward Snowden on their intricate global surveillance operations. It's fair to say they can read and understand much in this world or as a former CIA Director puts it, "When the fate of a nation and the lives of its soldiers are at stake, gentlemen do read each other's mail—if they can get their hands on it."

Lucky for those in IT industry, looking into mails is not necessary when trying to gain an edge, and may even be fruitless. I mean who uses the post office in the day of email, Twitter, Facebook, Snapchat and Slack. This doesn't mean though that quality intelligence gathering is not important. One may say, in the tech especially, it's one of the most important things you can do.

The tech industry is ubiquitous and all encompassing, in every region and in every conceivable type of business around the world, driving efficiency, cost cutting and improving lives. This means that everyone in the technology industry needs to have a good idea of what's happening, not just in the new fields of computational applications and architectural designs, but they must have an idea of go to market strategies, regional business forecasts, and industry swings. Senior leaders in tech need to know just about everything, globally. Sound pretty easy, right?

While tech does not have the power of an all seeing eye like the CIA's PRISM program, it does have something great: analysts. Analysts cover the spaces and the sectors that need to be known. Analysts have the years of experience needed to know when trends are happening. And, analysts need those in the tech field to get a good information on what's happening on the ground to go into their data stores. They are in the center of all things knowledge.

Having access to the analyst firms is only the first part of your intelligence journey, however, so you must work to use your time wisely. Garter, Forrester, IDC and the other numerous firms write on tech every day. Blogs, research, tweets, quotes in the media. There is an ocean to sift through but if you break it down into digestible portions, you may be able to fuse your knowledge with your pitch to win in the future. Here's some of those portions:

Competitive Reports
Magic Quadrant. Those two words strikes fear into the heart of many analyst

relations managers around the world, worried about their "dot" positioning. While positioning is important in Gartner's ubiquitous report (and in other firms such as the Forrester Wave, HfS Blueprint, etc.), dot placement is not the only thing that makes these reports so handy. Inside these reports is competitive insights that you cannot find anywhere else. They are line by line, platform by platform benchmarks that tell you exactly where you fall against your competition. In order to use these properly, you have to think "beyond the dot" and extrapolate this data properly, guiding your delivery teams with information on how they're performing and aiding your sales teams on how to position against competitors. Competitive reports give you a chance to test yourself against your peers. Make sure you don't just look at the 2×2's, and get to the heart of the analyst's views.

Deals Understanding and Forecasts

Famous futurist John Naisbitt once said "The most reliable way to forecast the future is to try to understand the present." We are very lucky that some analysts love to live on Excel charts and databases. By giving us a view of what's happening in the marketplace, month to month, quarter to quarter, these data analysts ensure that what we are hearing from our customers is matching to the broader market. Some firms such as Gartner and IDC offer great databases for deals information and forecasts by sector and technology. You can also reach out to advisory firms such as ISG or KPMG to keep you in the know. Remember that not every forecast and deal report is completely accurate. It's a relatively "get-it-close" science, so be sure to get a good field of view from your entire firm landscape before you go advising your senior leadership on your attack lines.

Go To Market Strategies

As we continue to enter an era where top notch industry consulting is paramount and technology becomes more and more of a commodity, it's never been more important to know how to communicate your platform or applications. Technology is complicated and never easy to describe when it comes to its roll out. Some analysts, normally insiders with rich industry experience or those that have been covering a particular domain for an eternity, know exactly what works when it comes to selling your product. Some firms have whole special series such as the Forrester Playbooks that gives readers a chance to look broadly over how to create visions, strategies, and operations to see your business humming. Meeting regularly with these analysts keeps your pitch perfect, so be sure to not only read but ask these analysts if pick up what you're putting down.

Webinars, Presentations, and Advisories

Most of the information analysts know is not in their papers; it's in their heads. Which is why getting to hear them speak live and interacting with them is some of the best Intel you can get. By scheduling timely advisory sessions with your key analysts, listening to them give a talk at a conference, or just listening to a webinar while you're sitting in traffic gives you a view that the screen might not be able to give you. If you can ask questions, please use this opportunity to probe a little deeper beyond their slides. One thing analysts love to do is share (that's what they get paid to do), so be sure to be prepared with some high quality questions that go into that next layer of information. Take quality notes, and perhaps, turn it into some media yourself, in internal blogs, an enterprise social reach out or an email to your group.

Social Listening and Media Benchmarking

This type of intelligence is half analysts work and half your own. Analysts' research, forecasts, and presentations can be perused, but don't forget your analysts more casual conversations: their blogs, LinkedIn articles, and Tweets. Sometimes this is where you get your leading edge info which hasn't had time to cook or received their research manager's approval. Make sure to follow all your analysts on Twitter and use a social listening platform like Radian6 or Synthesio to track what being said in the market and about you. Create an engine around paying attention to key analysts' blogs and make an effort to comment to keep the conversation happening. One other possibility is tracking your competition's thought leadership papers. Knowing what they are leading with in terms of their own white papers gives you a view of what they feel their strong suits are or where their next plays may be.

Internal Sales Data

One of the least used of all intelligence is something you already have: information from your own environment. Guys in the sales teams in the field and key delivery architects and engineers have just as much information as the analysts sometimes. Be sure to have weekly informal chats with your global teams on what's happening in the market. Pay attention to key metrics such as Win/Loss Reports and other internal benchmarks. Find out which competitors you are competing against the most, what technologies are winning deals, and what pitches are/are not working. Analyst Relations managers have unique positions in the company by viewing a firm at the highest level possible. Use this view as a catalyst of synthesis by working with a broad coalition of folks inside to get the best view outside.

The IT industry is a complicated and fast moving space. To win in the Intel game, you must work to be not only a knowledge seeker, but a maven, keen eyed tracker of all things around the world. Make sure you have a team dedicated to filtering all this noise into your program, and hopefully, you will see the wood from the trees. Or at least, some light out of the forest.

How To Use The Analyst Sales Impact Matrix

*T*he Analyst Sales Impact Matrix is one of the most-requested custom analyses produced by our Analyst Value Survey. Over the years, the AVS has gathered the opinions of thousands of users of analyst services about how they use analysts, and for what. The main report is a massive document, around 180 slides, but it does not answer every question. The Analyst Sales Impact Matrix shows which firms have the most influence on your firm's sales process. The Matrix shows each stage of the Buyer Decision Process, which was presented to the 2014 Analyst Relations Forum in the session led by Caroline Dennington and my colleague Samyr Jriri.

The Analyst Sales Impact Matrix narrows the focus onto the five or ten firms that are most influential over your target audience, in your target segments. We get that insight in either of two ways. Either companies using the main AVS pick the market areas that work for them, and we slice our data accordingly, or firms give us a list of their contacts and we conduct a customised study (normally of clients and prospects, but sometimes of the vendor's salespeople and other customer-facing staff). As you can see from the simplified sample above, the result is an influence mapping tool that can help focus and accelerate the sales cycle in several ways. Clients can use this

Analyst Sales Impact Matrix
Source: influencerelations.com/3762

© Kea Company 2015	Maintain awareness	Strategic planning	Budget planning	Research solutions	Solution needs	Evaluation & short-list	RFI/RFP & decision	Negotiate delivery
Big analyst firm a								
Freemium upstart b								
Big analyst firm c								
Niche leader d								
Sourcing advisor e								

Key	Low influence	Moderate influence	High influence	Highest influence

research in their sales enablement work, in sales training, to help management the implementation of alignment between communications, social and sales, to help reallocate effort between sales and AR, and to help sales and AR to work together to sell sales enablement projects internally.

Many people say that the particular advantage of their Matrix is the way that it can link AR up to specific points in the sales cycle. For example, after a product launch you might need to persuade colleagues to allow AR to streamline its efforts and focus on a subset of influencers for a while. In another setting, a sales team that's really fighting at one particular stage in the sales cycle might find that it needs to speak more with the influencers whose sweet spot that is.

Many firms want to keep the strategy and implementation of their sales enablement as much in-house as possible. However, they often lack the sort of hard data that goes into the Analyst Sales Impact Matrix. Few firms have the enormous volume of data that we collect through the Analyst Value Survey, and they certainly don't have our access to their competitor's clients. Furthermore, because Kea Company is the sole vendor of ARchitect Express (the contact management solution for the influencer industry) no-one has a more complete, or more up-to-date map of the influencers themselves. Kea's deep expertise in sales enablement also means that we have the business development skills and industry knowledge needed to let you hit the ground running with the Matrix.

How cool is it to be a Gartner Cool Vendor

*W*hat have Box, Dropbox, Nest, Evernote, Cloudera, Palantir and Instagram in common? They where all named a Cool Vendor by Gartner in the past five years.

So, what happened to the Cool Vendors?

We have surveyed the 1250+ tech companies that where nominated Cool Vendor by Gartner in the years 2009, 2010, 2011, 2012 and 2013. The reason for our survey is that we are interested to evaluate the impact the designations had on their business – and how they work with industry analysts.

Respondents are 193 CMOs and CEOs of these emerging technology companies from all over the world. A big thanks for their candor and collaboration! The results provide a unique view of the business impact and perception of analysts' value to emerging businesses.

Background for this is our big interest in the business value of Analyst Relations. So what is business value? In our opinion all investments a business makes in areas like influencer marketing, analyst services and analyst relations, in the end have to move the needle. Business value means more revenue, more cashflow, higher margins. That can be achieved by contributions to strategy, product development, marketing, sales, the ability to attract talent and capital. There is a chain of interactions and relationships behind this. And mutually beneficial relationships with industry analysts is one of the powerful factors.

Chicken or the egg

The question on your mind right now probably is, "were these companies cool before Gartner said they where, or is there a 'Gartner factor' here". Was it already a good company with above average potential or did it become better because analyst recognition? It is really hard to prove any causality there and we did not try to with this survey. However, the following results give an excellent impression of how the leadership of Cool Vendors has experienced the impact on their businesses.

Ecology of Cool Vendors

It is interesting to see which companies are independently growing, which have died and how many of the Cool Vendors are acquired. Cool Vendors operate in a very dynamic environment.

Just this week 2013 Cool Vendor MobileSpaces was acquired for a cool 100 million USD. Not bad for a firm founded in 2011.

Dead

Our research shows that 5% of the Cool Vendors doesn't exist anymore. Looking at startup success rate from venture capital, CV's have bigger success than the average young technology firm.

Eaten

Some 15% of the Cool Vendors have been acquired, including high profile acquisitions, such as Instagram, Yammer and Nest.

Most of the active acquirers are our usual suspects: Microsoft, Apple, Oracle, Salesforce, Juniper, Google, IBM and Facebook. These tech giants are often snapping up multiple Cool Vendors.

If we zoom in on the 2009 Cool Vendors which represent the oldest Cool Vendors we surveyed, there is an interesting pattern. In 2009 12% of the Cool Vendors was acquired. Almost a third (32%) of these acquisitions occurred in 2010, the year after the companies where nominated Cool Vendor. Another 23% of the acquisitions occurred in 2011, followed by 21% in 2012 and 12% in 2013. So there is a big spike in 2010, trending down in the following years.

Alive

Taking into account the numbers of failed and acquired Cool Vendors means that about 80% are still out there as independent companies, either private or public. Box has filed for an IPO, the likes of Dropbox, Evernote, Palantir reportedly pondering one. But it is also about the much smaller and less well known vendors punching above their weight.

What we asked the Cool Vendors

We asked the CMO's and CEO's of Cool Vendors:

▸ What did being named Cool Vendor (i.e. analyst recognition) bring your company?
▸ Was it a result of an Analyst Relations effort?
▸ What impact did being Cool Vendor have on sales, marketing, product development, attracting talent, attracting capital, business growth

Analyst Relations efforts

Analyst Relations definitely plays an important role for Cool Vendors. A quarter of respondents report having had proactive Analyst Relations efforts with Gartner in the year prior to becoming a Cool Vendor. And 28% say they were proactive in engaging other analysts as well.

Although 46% of the respondents said their analyst relations efforts in the year prior to becoming a Cool Vendor were purely reactive, 75% directly attribute their nomination to the ongoing Analyst Relations program they put in place. Three quarters of the leaders in these companies say AR directly led to

Did being named Cool Vendor resulted directly from your Analyst Relations programme?

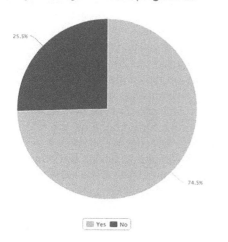

Which department benefitted the most from being named CV?

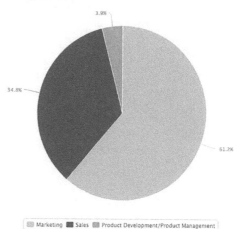

recognition. For AR professionals and tech vendor leadership, that is a very powerful conclusion.

Business impact

So what does that mean for a technology company, in terms of business impact? Some 65% report noticeable impact on the company's commercial success. The survey shows us there are obvious business functions that benefit from becoming a Cool Vendor:

1. **Marketing**
2. **Sales**
3. **Product development / Product management**

Since AR is often viewed as a part of marketing, the first place is obvious. Sales as the next logical field that benefits from analyst recognition. We see this interest, but also the struggle vendors have, in our practice at Kea Company, where over a third of our engagements are focused on sales enablement. 67% of Cool Vendors report that their sales force was enabled to be more effective and successful by the Cool Vendor nomination.

Do you feel that being named Cool Vendor enabled your sales force?

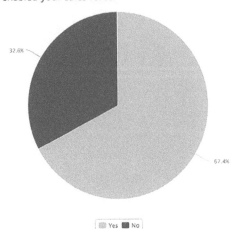

32.6%

57.4%

🟦 Yes 🔲 No

Attracting money and talent are areas where the business impact is less obvious according to our respondents. In both cases around 60% do not see an effect and around a third reporting some effect. You can look at impact on these areas as "second-order effects".

Growth and visibility in the market are two areas that substantially benefit from analyst recognition in the form of Cool Vendor nominations, with a quarter reporting quite a lot of effect on visibility. Almost a third contributes 5% or more of their business growth to being a Cool Vendor. With 4,5% even reporting over 15% of growth. These are numbers technology vendors should not ignore, or do so at their own peril. Analyst recognition leads to substantial business growth according to founders, Chief Executive Officers and Chief Marketing Officers of Gartner Cool Vendors!

The Skinny

More than half of the Cool Vendors have been mentioned in research by other analyst firms as a result of Analyst Relations efforts. Our respondents clearly say there is a positive relation between receiving accolades from industry analysts and quantitative (e.g. higher sales) as qualitative (e.g. more brand recognition) impact on their businesses.

This success doesn't come easy though. Most firms have a proactive approach to relationships with industry analysts. Building a relationship takes time and effort. It is like real life; no one met his or her partner and instantly had what we would call a relationship, let alone a deep and meaningful one. Dating, getting to know each other, spending time together and creating memories. We all know it takes two and a relationship is not something you take for granted. This is the romantic in me, but this analogy is oh so true for business relationships as well, especially with a crowd that is hard to please (sorry darling).

Our Point of View

We have chosen to research Gartner Cool Vendors because this is the best known and most consistent research program run in consecutive years, that is aimed to research a broad range of emerging technology areas and high potential companies, specifically including small and medium sized vendors. This time series and inclusion of tech firms in different stages of development and growth provide a spectacular view of up and coming tech firms and the impact that industry analysts can have.

Analyst Relations is a discipline that – if done well – can have a series of effects that lead to business growth and success. This survey of Cool vendors shows that. And it shows there is room for improvement, there is an opportunity that is under utilised. Firms can leverage Analyst Relations results better. Analyst Relations professionals have to learn how to tie AR outcomes to business outcomes.

That way CEOs, CMOs and other people in leadership positions at tech vendors can use analysts and AR better to reach the companies' full potential, quicker. Working with analysts can help to adopt an outside in perspective that is so important in today's customer experience focussed business ecosystem.

Tech vendors should notice this impact and realise that there are more analyst firms besides Gartner, way more. That means they have a lot more opportunities to create. Being aware of the benefits of mutually beneficial relationships with the relevant analysts is the first step. Setting up an Analyst Relations program that enables and drives these relationships is the next step.

If marketing and sales departments are capable of making the most of analyst recognition, tech vendors can really create competitive advantages that drive commercial success.

Key benefits of influencer marketing – it's not (only) about numbers

*W*hat is differentiating influencer marketing from the more conventional forms of marketing? Of course there are some things that influencer marketing has in common with traditional push marketing: It will help your company establish brand awareness and drive sales by generating contact points for your brand name and your products with the target audience. The main difference is how this is achieved. Influencer marketing does not rely on your ability (mainly defined by the depths of your pocket) to push the message towards the intended audience. Influencer marketing is all about establishing relations with those individuals and organisations that can act as multipliers for your messages.

But tweaking the numbers falls short of the potential benefits offered by a comprehensive influencer marketing strategy. There are several additional benefits that can be gained by interacting with the influencers in the market. For one thing the influencers typically represent the cutting edge regarding the trends in the market. This means by closely watching the influencers you can gain valuable insights for your own value proposition and messaging. If you manage to convince them to talk/write about your company or products there is a good chance that you are on the right track.

Another important factor is the credibility attributed to influencers by the market. This not only results in better qualified leads but also dramatically shortens the sales cycle since the prospect already places some trust in your offerings because of the approval from the influencer. In addition the likelihood of someone following a posted link from an influencer blog etc. is significantly higher than someone following a direct marketing link. This not only works with your target audience but also helps you with your influencer marketing efforts in general. Since most influencers will keep themselves informed about the latest developments and trends in their respective areas of interest your influence will keep growing at an exponential rate after establishing your first contact points within the "influencer community".

How Analysts influence the Buyer Decision Process

ymantec's EMEA comms leader Caroline Dennington and recent Gartner alum Samyr Jriri gave an impressive presentation at the Analyst Relations Forum 2014 about analysts' impact on sales. Context is key: analysts are increasingly stretched, something reflected by the increasing frequency with which some firms are taking complaints to Gartner's ombudsman, and making similar appeals at other firms.

Dennington, who previously led Symantec's global AR, explained that few AR people ask which analysts are really reviewing RFI and RFQ documents from customers, and getting more visibility into analyst impact allows firms to focus on developing closer relationships with top analysts. Analysts have a lot of flexibility, and often will recommend firms both inside and outside the Leader Quadrant: often quite unexpected firms can be added into consideration by analysts, even late in the process.

In the session, the speakers had an interactive discussion answering many pointed and specific questions from AR

Analysts Play a Key Role in All Stages of the Decision Making Process

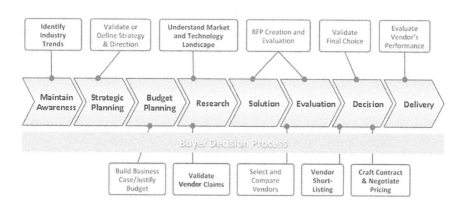

leaders about how to make the most of analysts' influence from day one through the deal cycle. One fascinating example picked up on Gartner Consulting, which has been involved in a deal where the relevant analyst is *not* involved in a relevant project: actually led by a consultant who that not so familiar with the market. Similarly to Gartner Consulting's insulation, Gartner also has a focussed group of analysts dealing with the investor market. They are often quite distant from the product analysts, and can usefully be a target for investor relations professionals. Gartner is also using 'stringers' who are not tenured analysts. but can be influential. Vendors' ability to help Gartner is limited, and many firms shared the frustration that Gartner does not interview, or even attempt to contact, all the customer references. If analysts are committed to using customers fully, reference-chasers at Gartner (In Europe that's Sally and her colleagues) can have a lot of influence on the research direction.

Flagship research like the Magic Quadrant and Forrester Wave are often painful. Thankfully Forrester's new automated tool for the Waves, which is now in beta, also tracks customer references and shows whether and when your customers were contacts.

Jriri, now a director at Kea Company, also stressed context. He gave several powerful examples of analyst influence on sales (even one deal won after the vendor took Gartner's advice to quadruple its prices) and stressed the fact that few purchases are influenced *only* by research. Analysts put their research into context, and buyers use multiple forms of research. He emphasised the complexity of Gartner in particular, and how few consultants and analysts will proactively reach out to clients or colleagues. The different people at Gartner following your market need to do their siloed job, and often only your client service rep will help you to navigate internally. Often Gartner analysts are rather uneven in their motivation, or ability, to connect with (or even find) Gartner consultants working on deals in the analysts' market.

There was a vibrant discussion about how independent and impartial advisory and consulting specialists can be. Some firms have a noted reputation for independence, however other advisory teams are less transparent. As Ed Gyurko noted, advisory consultants are quite generally less transparent than industry analysts. Samyr broadened the context to talk about influencer relations, making it an astonishingly broad session which also drilled down into a lot of specifics.

Using Analyst Written Research: Bad Practices

The IT industry analysts do a good job of researching and analysing the IT industry. Where they often do not do a good job lies in educating their own clients on how to use the research and recommendations. This is critical because analyst clients could end up making wrong decisions about technology and services, putting their companies – and their jobs – at risk. Don't take written research at face value or view only the research from a single firm.Unfortunately, time-constrained consumers tend to bad practices such as:

▶ Using old, out-of-date research about markets, vendors and products. While what constitutes "old" varies with market any research paper more than three months old should be checked to see if it is the most current.

▶ Using the recommendations in a research paper without knowing the assumptions used to make those recommendations.

▶ Using information or recommendations out-of-context. Most published research papers are part of a series of published materials that provide context to the recommendations that may appear in any single paper. Vendors may also provide an analyst chart or quote in a sales presentation and the entire report should be reviewed.

▶ Using generic information that does not necessarily relate to the company's situation.

▶ Using material about a vendor that is from a related but different market coverage.

▶ A good research consumer will review materials from multiple firms for consistency, immediacy, applicability, and relevance and then check with the analyst(s) directly to enhance their understanding.

Bottom Line: The most important tool to leverage in using analyst research is the telephone. While the published research is useful, the real value of an analyst subscription lies in being able to talk directly with the analysts to apply the research to your specific situation. Whenever using an analyst to make a product or vendor decision, it is important to set up a series of inquiries validate your perception of the current research.

Building Credibility to Boost Sales with IT Analyst Relations

hen talking to IT vendors eager to grow their business I usually come across a number of common challenges they face. One of the biggest issues which lies outside the companies (as opposed to e. g. finance requirements to fund the growth or adding enough skilled people to their workforce) is that once they are moving out of their comfort zone they are facing prospects that are much more skeptical than those in their home markets.

It seems to be a common pattern that vendors manage to grow to a certain size (depending on the size of their home market this is often somewhere between five and twenty million dollars) and then start thinking about ways to expand further. This often is when they are confronted with the 'real outside world' for the first time. Before this they managed to successfully leverage their network, or simply were the vendor with an office location closest to where the customer was. This kind of home advantage usually works up to a certain point. You might be able to successfully sell to new clients based on recommendations from your network to 2nd degree connections but that's about where it stops. When you are dealing with prospects who have never heard of you and who don't have any other obvious connection path (be it geographically or personal) to your company the selling gets much tougher. Obviously the first thing any vendor will do is to bring his USPs to the attention of the potential buyer. But be honest: How many competitors are out there who are making similar claims in regards to their or their solution's capabilities? At this stage it doesn't matter if their (or your) claims are true because at this stage the only thing that matters is the question of who is going to get the chance to proof their claims either by further demonstrations, POCs, trials or ideally by closing the deal.

A similar challenge vendors are facing is connected to the deal size. A lot of customers are willing to 'risk' a limited amount of money on a new vendor or a solution that is new to the market. With increasing deal size this inclination to take some risk quickly declines which is why smaller or new vendors often fail to win the larger deals in the market. This is also true in regards to the 'business criticality' of a solution. Buying something that is a nice to have from a new vendor is much easier than buying a solution that is business critical or security relevant from an unproven source.

Credibility wins business.

With markets where there are typically multiple vendors offering multiple solutions for a problem the buyer needs to significantly narrow down the field of potential suppliers. So being on the short list for further evaluation must be the primary goal in the early stage of the sales process. This is where the topic of credibility comes into play. When competing in their home markets a vendor is virtually guaranteed to get a place on the short list. Once competing outside: Not so much. Credibility means that a potential customer has enough trust in the claims you make about your company and your solution to give you the chance

to prove yourself. Having credible sales people goes a long way towards that goal but obviously they are very hard to find. In addition some customers will never accept anything coming directly from a vendor at face value. Also references help to generate trust, even though the effectiveness of a reference quickly declines when they are not meeting the criteria a specific customer is looking for. This can include the requirement for a reference from the same country, the same vertical or of similar size – or ideally all of this at the same time. And of course if you were not lucky enough to acquire the right mix of reference customers in your home market this only brings you back to the initial problem of getting new customers in the first place. So the question remains how to best handle the credibility issue.

Influencers create credibility

This is where influencer relations has its place in the marketing mix. People like journalist and industry analysts make their living from evaluating technologies, vendors and solutions. Industry analysts in particular are heavily involved in advising technology buyers in regards to their vendor selection and short list creation. With industry analyst groups such as Gartner, Forrester, IDC and Ovum influencing between 40% and 60% of commercial technology sales their market reach is much bigger than anything a midsize vendor can hope to achieve on its own. This means that being mentioned by analysts – either in written research or in 1:1 inquiries – will open up indirect access to many potential customers. Coverage in official research publications is the most powerful tool for your sales people and your marketing materials to demonstrate that your technology, company, products and service offerings and methods are highly recognized and credible.

Analysts are writing about your market, whether you like it or not. Being pro-active in reaching out to analysts gives you the strategic advantage of being able to influence their research by providing them with the insight they need, when they need it. Analyst Relations is not a billion dollar club. It is critical that analysts are well informed of your company strategy, products, and services. This needs to be an ongoing process to maintain a top-of-mind status, especially for a vendor that aims for higher name recognition and company growth. Early engagement with analysts is a great way to get analyst buy-in and top-of-mind presence to increase credibility and in turn to secure your place on the short list and to boost sales.

Appendix

The Magic Quadrant and Tech Vendors

Don't Obsess, Don't Ignore (Part One)

*E*ven with a host of blogs and other forms of social media, Gartner's Magic Quadrant remains the IT market's most highly visible piece of commentary. Because the Magic Quadrant impacts billions of dollars of corporate IT purchases, some tech vendor executives put too much emphasis on "moving the dot", which drains resources from the overall AR plan. Other vendors decide to ignore Magic Quadrants, missing an opportunity to leverage an effective marketing channel. Neither approach is 100% appropriate. In this post, we provide background on the Magic Quadrant and suggest that vendors take a middle approach between obsession and indifference.*

It is not uncommon for our strategists to hear the following comment from an Analyst Relations (AR) manager: "Our execs – or even board of directors – have made improving our position on the Magic Quadrant **THE** (not 'a') goal for AR." While ignoring the Magic Quadrant (MQ) can be perilous to a vendor's top line, too much emphasis on a MQ can drain scarce AR resources from influencing all the analysts covering your particular market. The downside is that AR won't be able to develop counterbalancing relationships with analysts in other firms, leaving the vendor dangerously reliant on Gartner and the MQ for positive analyst coverage.

We think it's time that vendors take a balanced approach to the MQ.

Snapshot of the Magic Quadrant

The MQ is the most famous and enduring industry analyst signature research. It was developed by Gideon Gartner, Mike Braude and Doug Cayne in mid-1980s based on Boston Consulting Group's "2 by 2" graphic from the 1960's. The purpose is to offer a snapshot – not a definitive view – of a technology market. It acts as a visual "Strategic Planning Assumption" tool and covers all markets: software, hardware, services.

Around 1993, Gartner's Editorial Department unilaterally decided that it would no longer permit analysts to use the phrase "Magic Quadrant" to describe this research graphics on the grounds that it was neither a quadrant nor magic. Needless to say, this caused an uproar throughout Gartner, especially in the Sales force. Why?

The MQ truly is magic… for Gartner

The MQ is branding, marketing and selling magic for Gartner. Even in the early 90's it was becoming legendary. While Gideon Gartner bemoans the dominance and misuse of the MQ, it is valued by the IT executives that use it every day.

Yes, the Magic Quadrant can impact billions of dollars of IT purchasing decisions. Often it is used to select which vendors can bid on a particular project, either formally (e.g., only Leaders are added to a short list) or informally (e.g., the IT decision makers think "hmm, this vendor doesn't have that great of a position on the MQ so let's just leave it off the short list").

However, even though it is pervasive and has a high impact, the MQ is not the only game in town. Other analyst firms (e.g., Forrester with its Wave) have high visibility research deliverables. Furthermore, even though Gartner is the largest analyst firm, not every buyer of technology is a client of Gartner. Gartner's CEO Gene Hall often says on their quarterly earnings call that it is only in approximately 20% of global enterprises with US$1 billion or more in revenues. And even in those clients, Gartner has not penetrated every part of the company. Finally, Gartner is not influential in every market covered by a MQ.

▸ Are you having trouble convincing your executives to take the middle approach between obsession and indifference? Kea Company's insight on the Magic Quadrant can be a valuable tool in your education campaign about the appropriate approach to take.

Kea Company Technique

- Investigate how the Magic Quadrant actually impacts your market segment
- Educate your executives about the real role of the Magic Quadrant in your market and with your customers and prospects
- Develop, communicate and execute a plan on an appropriate campaign to change or maintain your company's position(s) on the relevant Magic Quadrant(s)

Bottom Line

While Gartner's Magic Quadrant is the signature IT analyst deliverable and has tremendous influence with buyers of technology products and services, IT vendors should not become obsessed with moving their dots. It is critical that executives and AR managers take a realistic appraisal of their situation in regards to any particular MQ and devote only the amount of effort proportional to the potential return.

Three Common Mistakes (Part Two)

For a variety of reasons, communications and IT vendor Analyst Relations and executives make a number of mistakes concerning the Gartner Magic Quadrant (MQ) and how their companies should react to it. Decision makers at IT vendors need to take a step back and carefully consider the appropriate level of effort to put into "moving the dot."

The first mistake is proceeding without understanding how your prospects and customers/clients value and use the MQ. You should be surveying your customer/clients and prospects about **which research firms and reports they use.**

The second mistake is assuming that you know what the underlying market-specific criteria and assumptions are for the MQ without talking to the appropriate analysts. Repositioning your "dot" on a Magic Quadrant doesn't happen just because you have a great product or service. **Often the most important criteria are not captured in written format and do not focus on features/functions.** In order to proceed, it is important that the vendor talk to analysts to find out all the criteria and proof points needed to meet those criteria.

The third mistake made is to let the tail wag the dog. While the Magic Quadrant is a key research deliverable, you can best impact your position by developing and maintaining a **solid relationship with the analysts** and providing the the education they need to fully understand your company and your products and services.

While these three mistakes are very important, there are other mistakes that AR teams need to watch out for:

1. **Waiting for the analyst to contact you**
2. **Not staying on top of evolving criteria and assumptions**
3. **Not staying on top of changing publishing schedules**
4. **Not understanding the importance of a change in analyst ownership of a Magic Quadrant**
5. **Not trying to change the criteria and assumptions used to create the Magic Quadrant**
6. **Not treating each Magic Quadrant as a separate entity if the vendor is on multiple, related Magic Quadrants**
7. **Not countering competitors' efforts at influencing criteria or positioning**
8. **Bashing the analyst, Gartner or Magic Quadrant**
9. **Going to the analysts' manager or Gartner execs**
10. **Going to Gartner's Vendor Relations department**
11. **Going on "autopilot" when dealing with the analyst**

* *Are you having trouble convincing your executives about the typical mistakes that vendors make? Kea Company's insights on the Magic Quadrant can be a valuable tool in your education campaign about the appropriate approach to take with the MQ. Feel free to request a critique of your MQ plans to ensure the appropriate effort to carry out realistic goals.*

Kea Company Technique:

▶ AR managers need to take zero-based evaluation of their MQ plans to ensure that they are realistic

▶ AR managers need to be watchful that their programs are not falling into one of the common mistakes about the MQ

▶ AR teams need to educate their executives about the common mistakes and steps to avoid them

Bottom Line: There are a number of mistakes concerning the MQ that AR teams need to be concerned about, not all of which are listed in this post. AR managers need to take a balanced approach to the MQ, **neither giving it more attention than it deserves nor providing insufficient resources to "moving the dot."**

Unleash your inner Sherlock (Part Three)

Warning: Homework ahead! It is critical for AR to thoroughly research a particular Magic Quadrant and its history. Even AR staffs that have been working with Gartner on a MQ for a long time could benefit from doing a little digging into the background of the MQ in order to separate reality from faulty memory and myth.

Kea Company Technique:

Check on past Magic Quadrants – The first task is to obtain past versions of the Magic Quadrants. You can search Gartner's research database, but frankly you still have to ask. While Gartner analysts published dozens of distinct Magic Quadrants in the traditional Research Note format every year, there are so many publishing platforms at Gartner (e.g., presentations and toolkits) that a MQ can show up in either as an original piece of research or a reprint of something published earlier. Because not all presentations are included in Gartner's research database, it is necessary for you to call up the relevant Gartner analyst and ask. In addition, ask for publications that have supporting content about the MQ and market criteria.

Non-clients can use Gartner Sales to assist you in getting to speak to an analyst. Use the argument that by knowing which Magic Quadrants you are on, you will be better able to justify future investments in Gartner services in order to gain Sales' assistance. In either case, ask for MQs that were published in Research Notes and other formats. By the way, non-clients can search Gartner research database for Research Notes with Magic Quadrants. While this does not give you access to the analysts, buying individual Research Notes is a means to gather some needed information, but frankly is so expensive that it is not worth it. Before pulling out your credit card, you should check the Internet for a free copy of the MQ courtesy of a vendor website. The vast majority of MQs are licensed for reprint by vendors for marketing purposes and it only takes a little searching to find MQs.

As part of your research check the Gartner Research Methodologies page, which can provide you with some insight on the schedule and the general methodologies.

Once you have gathered all the MQs and supporting content, analyze* them for:

▶ Rough publishing schedule
▶ Marketplace definition
▶ Evolution of criteria
▶ Changing analyst coverage

Kea Company clients can schedule an inquiry to discuss how to analyze the relevant published content for insights into the direction a MQ is heading.

Bottom Line: It is important for AR teams to do their homework to stay on top of evolving criteria and assumptions. Assuming that you know what the important underlying criteria and assumptions are for the Magic Quadrant without talking to analysts can result in work to create proof points for your company that does not matter. Just reading the Research Notes is not sufficient, as the most important criteria are often not captured in written format.

Homework questions:

Question: Are your executives too much on either extreme of the obsess-and-ignore spectrum? Have you attempted to move them to the center?

Question: Do you have regular calls with analysts in charge of relevant MQs to determine how they perceive the market is changing and how this will impact the criteria for a MQ?

Talk to the Analyst (Part Four)

It is critical for Analyst Relations (AR) to thoroughly research a particular Magic Quadrant and its history. Even AR staffs that have been working with Gartner on a MQ for a long time could benefit from doing a little digging into the background of the MQ in order to separate reality from faulty memory and myth.

Kea Company Technique:

Talk with the analyst – Obviously, AR should be interacting with their Tier 1 analysts on a regular basis on a number of issues. In many cases being in charge of a MQ means automatic Tier 1 status for a Gartner analyst. Many of those interactions will provide valuable insights into the MQ and the analyst's criteria for it. However, there needs to be a dedicated call on the MQ* that occurs once a quarter. Topics to be covered include:

▸ Changes in the analyst's responsibility, new additions to the team, both creation and peer review
▸ If you are on a Magic Quadrant with more than one author, what

is the current relationship between the multiple authors and how is that evolving? Will that impact your position?

▶ Changes in criteria, weights and assumptions
▶ Analyst's vision for the market
▶ Whether new MQs will be created that overlap this space
▶ Next publication date and format
▶ What you have to do to move in desired direction
▶ What the competition is doing to leapfrog you
▶ Danger signs
▶ Strengths and weaknesses of the players on the Magic Quadrant
▶ Necessary proof points to meet criteria.

A tricky insight to obtain from analysts is the team dynamics. Often you have to approach this issue indirectly.

During these MQ intelligence-gathering calls, do not argue with the analyst about your company, your products, position or criteria. Because these are regular quarterly calls you don't want the analyst to feel uncomfortable when they see it on their calendar. Nor do you want the analyst to act defensively during the call. Rather use this call to gather needed information that will help you plan future interactions. After each quarterly call, you should send an e-mail to the analyst documenting what you heard. This will provide an **audit trail** in case there are disagreements in the future about whether or not your company should have a more favourable positioning on the next MQ.

* Kea Company clients can schedule an inquiry to help you prepare for your quarterly analyst calls and then analyze what you heard.

Bottom Line: It is important for AR teams to do their **homework** to stay on top of evolving criteria and assumptions. Assuming that you know what the important underlying criteria and assumptions are for the Magic Quadrant without talking to analysts can result in work to create proof points for your company that does not matter. Just reading the Research Notes is not sufficient, as the most important criteria are often not captured in written format. Savvy AR professionals will be in frequent contact with the analyst seeking intelligence about the market in order to anticipate changes in criteria and assumptions.

Question: *Do you have regular calls with analysts in charge of relevant MQs to determine how they perceive the market is changing and how this will impact the criteria for a MQ?*

Moving The Dot (Part Five)

*R*epositioning your 'dot' on a Gartner Magic Quadrant does not happen just because you have a great product or service. It takes information, a plan, Analyst Relations execution and avoiding mistakes.

Expanding Your Goals – Moving the dot should not be the only goal of every analyst interaction. AR teams and spokespeople should insure that you accomplish your goal of moving the dot while working on other aspects of your analyst relationship such as competitive intelligence gathering, relationship building, training a novice analyst, strategy review, etc. Rarely will a vendor be interested in accomplishing one goal when interacting with the Gartner analyst in charge of a MQ. Some goals specifically concerning the MQ include:

▶ Moving your dot, either up or to the right or both

▶ Moving your competitors' dots either down or to the left or both

- Increasing the distance between you and competitors
- Preventing your competitors from leapfrogging you
- Increasing the distance between you and a line separating the blocks
- Influencing the analyst's underlying criteria and assumptions to reinforce your position and put your competitors at a disadvantage
- Influencing the definition of what is the market being covered
- Creating a new MQ

Kea Company Technique:
- Do your homework
- Talk to the analyst
- Determine whether or not the results will be worth the effort
- Set up near term and long term goals for each MQ
- Set up an Action Plan for each Magic Quadrant
- Educate management to get buy-in and prevent complacency
- Execute
- Do not become complacent

* Kea Company clients can obtain the outline for "Influence Recurring Research Reports — Research Action Plan". Advisory clients can also set up one or more inquiries to go through the content, review draft plans, brief executives on the MQ and moving the dot, coach spokespeople on dealing with Gartner analysts, role play the analyst in preparation for inquiries and briefings and act as a sounding board.

Bottom Line: While moving the dot does require a significant amount of effort, it is an achievable goal with the right approach. However, AR managers need to evaluate whether the potential movement is worth the resources and then manage executive expectations in order to obtain a realistic level of support.

Question: *Do you use a standard plan for laying out a campaign to change your position on a Magic Quadrant?*

The Danger is Complacency (Part Six)

There is a certain amount of self congratulations that occur when a vendor achieves a favorable "Leader" position on a Magic Quadrant. Because they are in the "Leaders" block, vendors feel like their job is complete. The problem is that such an attitude could lead to complacency and endanger a company's coveted status in the future. Vendors in this situation could receive a nasty surprise as competitors leapfrog them or as they slip into the Challengers or Visionaries blocks.

This is not only a problem with "Leaders" since vendors in the "Challengers" and "Visionaries" blocks also feel that they can rest on their laurels. Most surprising are "Niche" vendors who are happy merely to be mentioned on a Magic Quadrant. The messages in this post are directed to Leaders, but also apply to all vendors, no matter what their position on the MQ.

What is the Danger? We've witnessed vendors go from the best Leaders position in a Magic Quadrant only to slide to the Challengers block in the next version. Why? The vendor had become complacent about briefing the analyst and missed that the "bar" for inclusion in the Leaders block was being raised. They had what it took to continue being a leader, but had failed to communicate that to the analyst. So what happed was:

▶ They didn't stay on top of evolving criteria and assumptions
▶ They didn't continue to improve the appropriate level of communications with the analyst
▶ Their approach to the analyst and the information used became stale
▶ They didn't understand the implications of changing analyst coverage
▶ They didn't counter their competitors' attempts to influence the analyst

Kea Company Technique:
Do a Zero-based Rethink about your Magic Quadrant Influence Efforts — We recommend that vendors ask themselves tough questions about their current MQ approach and answer them honestly. The more questions you answer in the negative the more likely you will wake up to a nasty surprise the next time the Magic Quadrant is updated. Use the insights from the MQ approach evaluation to change your MQ plan if necessary.

Bottom Line: The primary problem for vendors in the Leaders block on one of Gartner's Magic Quadrants is complacency about their position. Savvy vendors combat this complacency by **never being satisfied with their current position** and supporting commentary. This attitude leads these vendors to constantly evaluate their approach and work to improve their plans and execution.

Equipping Sales for the MQ Effect (Part Seven)

Gartner's Magic Quadrant can have a powerful impact on IT vendor sales cycles – anointing some vendors as a prime candidate for a sales opportunity while denying other vendors even a chance to bid. In order to exploit positive placement on a Magic Quadrant and mitigate negative placement, vendor sales executives need to work with AR to prepare and train their sales teams on certain basics about the Magic Quadrant. To a large extent the Magic Quadrant is just another form of analyst research that sales reps have to take into account when working with customers and prospects. However, the MQ does have some unique aspects that have to be addressed including:

- **Multiple MQs** – A vendor can be on any number of MQs, which increases the chances that a prospect will be using wrong research
- **Out-of-date MQs** – Earlier versions of a MQ can be available for a long time, which can put a vendor with an improved position at a disadvantage
- **Four boxes, four responses** – How a sales responds to or uses a MQ is different depending on which box the vendor is in, which complicates training and Silver Bullets
- **IT managers who mis-use the MQ** – Vendors will find that their prospects do not know how to use the MQ, which means developing techniques that diplomatically teach prospects how to apply the MQ
- **IT managers with MQs but not inquiry access to Gartner analysts** – Prospects can get MQ reprints from vendor websites or sales reps without being clients of Gartner, which increases the likelihood of the prospect mis-using the MQ without giving the sales rep the option of suggesting the prospect call the Gartner analyst
- **Proliferating or changing MQs** – Gartner is adding, retiring and changing MQs on a regular basis, which increases the chance that a prospect is using the wrong MQ.

Vendors covered by one or more Magic Quadrants should ensure that their AR-Sales Partnership Program* takes into account the unique characteristics of the MQ.

* Kea Company has the AR-Sales Partnership Plan Builder (a full day workshop) that helps vendors develop comprehensive plans for how AR supports Sales. Clients can use inquiry to review their AR-Sales Partnership Program plan to ensure that it appropriately takes into account the special aspects of the MQ.

Bottom Line: In general, responding to situations in which a MQ is impacting a sales cycle is not much different than responding to any other piece of analyst research. The primary difference is that, unlike much research put out by the hundreds of analyst firms, the Magic Quadrant cannot be ignored. Savvy vendors will proactively address how MQs can impact sales deals – for the good or bad – and put into place processes and resources that assist the Sales force in dealing with the influence of Gartner's Magic Quadrant.

The Consumers' Guide to the Magic Quadrant

IT managers: it's never, ever, only about the upper-right dot when it comes to Forrester Waves or Gartner Magic Quadrants

One of the things that drive vendors – and even some Gartner and Forrester analysts – crazy is when an IT buyer zeros in on the vendors in the upper right-hand corner of a Forrester Wave or Magic Quadrant to the exclusion of all other vendors. It is human nature to go for the most obvious choices. IT buyers often find it simpler to select those who they initially perceive as top in their market. Sadly, that is not how analysts want those highly-visible research graphics to be used. Instead IT managers should be looking to align their company's product or services requirements with the criteria that underlie any particular Wave or Quadrant. Only after considering those conditions should managers make a decision about which vendors to add to a short list.

Here is a typical example of how buyers can misuse the Forrester Wave. An IT buyer made a decision about which vendors to include on a bid worth several hundreds of millions of US dollars solely based on which vendors were the most up, and to the right, on a Forrester Wave. They did not mind that other vendors were also rated "Leaders." This particular Forrester client thought that only upper right-hand dots were worthy of consideration. This choice not only caused consternation in the unselected vendors, but also did not provide the buyer with the best possible solution.

The Forrester Wave and the Gartner Magic Quadrant are the IT analyst industry's signature research deliverables. They, and charts like them, impact billions of dollars of corporate IT purchases every year. Unfortunately, none of the major analyst firms does a good enough job of educating the consumers of these diagrams, most of whom are not their clients, on how to use the research and recommendations. This duty should be taken more seriously by analyst firms because users of analyst research often end up making poor decisions about technology and services: they put companies and jobs at risk.

For several years, Gartner had the following disclaimer in Magic Quadrant research notes: "[The Magic Quadrant] depicts Gartner's analysis of how certain vendors measure against criteria for that marketplace, as defined by Gartner. Gartner does not endorse any vendor, product or service depicted in the Magic Quadrant, and does not advise technology users to select only those vendors placed in the "Leaders" quadrant."

One problem is that in many cases, this disclaimer was in small print at the end of a long research note, where it is almost certainly not to be read by many. More importantly, Gartner seems to have dropped the disclaimer in 2013.

Occasionally analyst firms will publish documents that try to give context. After

2001, we were able to point clients to a Gartner note by Jess Thompson about what he repeatedly called 'Panning for Gold': looking outside the Leaders Quadrant of Gartner's Magic Quadrant. In his second note on Panning for Gold, in 2007, Jess wrote: "In certain cases, you should consider products from vendors that aren't in the Leaders quadrant. If you work hard enough and look in the right places, then you may find "golden nugget" vendors elsewhere." That said, Gartner has placed both Thompson's notes in its archive. Even when they were live, the metaphor of Panning for Gold suggested to many users that the while they could find good options outside the MQ, it could be time-consuming and unsuccessful.

In August 2017, Gartner refreshed a 2014 note called "How Markets and Vendors Are Evaluated in Gartner Magic Quadrants". The authors are managers, rather than analysts: two MVPs, David Black and Julie Thomas, and Tim Weaver, director for content strategy. The authors write: "We do not recommend evaluating vendors in the Leaders quadrant only, and ignoring those in other quadrants. There are many reasons for this, including that a vendor in the Niche Players quadrant could offer functions that are ideally suited to your needs. Similarly, a Leader may not offer functions that meet your requirements — for example, its offerings may cost more than those of its competitors', or it may not support your region or industry."

These notes of guidance seem useful, but they will have a few modest effect compared to a disclaimer placed in each Magic Quadrant.

So what should a diligent IT buyer do to make sure they are using these research deliverables correctly? Ideally, you should call and talk to the analyst, although many analysts might make themselves available only to their most valuable clients. Even so, the most powerful tool to leverage in handling analyst research is the telephone. While their published analysis is useful, analysts create their highest value comes when they can talk directly with professionals who want to apply it to a company's specific situation. Whenever using an analyst to make a product or vendor decision, it is best practice to set up a series of inquiries to:

▸ Provide background on your company and systems' requirements
▸ Ensure that you are using the right Magic Quadrant or Forrester Wave – the most recent and in the right market
▸ Obtain the criteria and assumptions used by the analyst in creating their MQs or Waves
▸ Procure copies of both unpublished (e.g., conference presentations) and published research that provides supporting information
▸ Discuss applying the MQ or Wave within the context of the company's situation.

However, before calling the analyst with an inquiry, there are a few steps that need to be accomplished to make the session efficient and effective.

It is more difficult to get into these discussions if you are not a client of the analyst firm. Often a vendor can license reprint rights to a supportive Magic Quadrant or Wave to post on its website so more people can download it, but those readers might not subscribe to the analyst firm themselves. In this case, it is essential that you do not add the vendor to your shortlist based on the MQ or Wave without the right context. In particular, remember that vendors chose to reprint research that puts them in the best light, and they spend on adverts and search engine optimization with the hope that you will find that sympathetic report rather than more neutral analysis.

Bottom Line: Forrester's Wave and Gartner's Magic Quadrant can be a useful component of a product or service selection process. However, neither research deliverable should be used as the sole basis for selecting vendors for a short list. It is crucial that IT buyers conduct due diligence to understand the underlying criteria and information that went into the research graphic. Even more critical is that the IT buyers talk to the analyst to apply the research to their company's situation.

Question: *For IT buyers – Are you aware of this process for ensuring the correct use of the Magic Quadrant or Wave? Do you look for vendors beyond the "Leaders" box? For vendors – Have you ever been excluded from a sales opportunity because you thought the IT buyer was not using the research deliverable correctly?*

Are you getting the most from your analyst contracts? We can help. Our strategists can:

▸ Evaluate the usage of your contracted analyst services and suggest ways to maximize business value from your investment
▸ Train your colleagues on making the most of analyst access
▸ Critique your upcoming analyst contracts to ensure you are getting the right services from the right firms to meet your business needs
▸ Save you time, money and aggravation

To learn more, email ***duncan.chapple@kearesearch.com*** or telephone ***+44 20 7993 8655***.